Caged in Chaos

A Dyspraxic Guide to Breaking Free

Victoria Biggs

Illustrated by Sharon Tsang

With a foreword by Jamie Hill

Jessica Kingsley Publishers
London and Philadelphia

First published in 2005
by Jessica Kingsley Publishers
116 Pentonville Road
London N1 9JB, UK
and
400 Market Street, Suite 400
Philadelphia, PA 19106, USA

www.jkp.com

Library of Congress Cataloging in Publication Data
Biggs, Victoria.
Caged in chaos : a dyspraxic guide to breaking free / Victoria Biggs.
p. cm.
ISBN-13: 978-1-84310-347-9 (pbk.)
ISBN-10: 1-84310-347-8 (pbk.)
1. Apraxia—Popular works. I. Title.
RC394.A75B535 2005
616.85'52—dc22

2004030441

British Library Cataloguing in Publication Data
A CIP catalogue record for this book is available from the British Library

ISBN 978 1 84310 347 9

Printed and Bound in Great Britain by
Athenaeum Press, Gateshead, Tyne and Wear

Contents

Queer little twists and quirks go into the making of an individual. To suppress them all and follow clock and calendar and creed until the individual is lost in the neutral grey of the host is to be less than true to our inheritance...life, that gorgeous quality of life, is not accomplished by following another man's rules. It is true we have the same hungers and the same thirsts, but they are for different things and in different ways and in different seasons... Lay down your own day, follow it to its noon, your own noon, or you will sit in an outer hall listening to the chimes but never reaching high enough to strike your own.

Angelo Patri, quoted in A Beautiful Mind,
Sylvia Nasar

For Grandma, with love

Foreword

'Sit down, Bluey, and shut up.'
'They're all the same, you know – stinking blue-eyes.'
'Thick as planks, the lot of them.'

In the 1960s an American elementary school teacher tried out an experiment on her young class. In the aftermath of the death of the racial equality campaigner, Martin Luther King, she decided to show the children what it felt like to be discriminated against. Nowadays such an experiment would be seen as cruel, especially when the subjects are so young, but maybe that is only because of the horrific consequences...

Jane Elliott split up her class according to their eye colour, proclaiming brown-eyed children to be more intelligent, fit and well-behaved – a master race. Blue-eyed children were derided, mocked and made to wear collars to distinguish them from their betters. Within a few days the brown-eyed children had become frighteningly bigoted. Sure of their own superiority, they took every opportunity to abuse the blue-eyes.

This is all interesting, but what relevance does it have to Vicky's book?

Well, the relevance lies within an often-overlooked result from Elliott's work. When the brown-eyes were convinced of their own superiority, their work dramatically improved and they answered questions Elliott knew they would never have attempted to do before. Meanwhile, the work of their blue-eyed classmates declined in quality – things they used to be able to do with comparative ease they now found impossibly difficult.

Books are very dangerous things – particularly those that focus on disability, even when they do so in a light-hearted and anecdotal style. Dyspraxia affects people in vastly different ways – some people find it difficult to sit in a chair without falling over, whilst others have no trouble ice-skating; a lot of sufferers have difficulty with mathematics, but a brief search on some dyspraxia websites will reveal others studying for maths degrees at universities. Dyspraxia is unique in every person.

I think it's about time I introduced myself. I am not dyspraxic – I don't even have a related condition. I have even argued (half-heartedly) that dyspraxia doesn't exist at all. I can only assume that at least one of the points that I have made in my heated 'discussions' with the author has some merit, in order for her to have allowed me to write this.

It seems customary for foreword writers to make some inspirational speech about the subject of the book, but I don't think this one has *a* subject. The sufferers of dyspraxia seem to be so diverse that it would be impossible to talk about them as one entity – which is lucky, as it would be hypocritical of me to try to talk about dyspraxia in any insightful way.

However, I can talk about the author.

It is a testament to her strength of character that she went for so long without any official recognition of her problem, but perhaps it is the lateness of her diagnosis that has made her so obsessive about dyspraxia – too obsessive for my liking. I would love to praise her efforts, but I am so used to telling her that dyspraxia is a minor thing that I couldn't do so in good heart. Vicky has in the past told me that her very severe dyspraxia affects her ability to judge the depths of swimming pools, tie her shoelaces or, when trying to drive, to keep the car in the centre of the road. This worries me, as I – and in two of the cases, most of the human race – struggle with these very same things!

So when you read of the author's struggles against tin openers, or her eternal battle against stairs, remember the children in Jane Elliott's class, and the difference self-belief can make. Don't let a list of symptoms dictate who you are. I wish you a good read.

Jamie Hill

A note from the author

Jamie is a fellow-student in my year at school. When I asked him for permission to include some of his more unorthodox views in my book, to say he was a bit on the surprised side would be an understatement. He was unable to work out why I wanted to open *Caged in Chaos* with a tirade that I seemingly completely disagree with. My reasoning is woven into the fabric of this book, but to save him – and you – the trouble of unravelling it, I will give it here.

I've met dozens of kind, comforting people who accept my description of my condition without argument – they are perfectly nice, perfectly sympathetic, and perfectly understanding. Yet they weren't the ones who helped my bewildered dyscalculic brain to study for my GCSE maths exam. That was Jamie the sceptic. He wouldn't let me use the words 'dyspraxia' or 'dyscalculia' to justify my inability to write a number three the right way round, but he conceded that I needed help – and he gave it. Although I definitely (and vociferously!) disagree with his belief that my problems are shared by most of the population, I was deeply touched by his exhortation not to 'let a list of symptoms dictate who you are'. If you have dyspraxia, please remember that there is a lot more to you as a person than an unusual Greek word. Use the label, but don't be defined by it.

CHAPTER 1

A Recipe for Chaos

Out of order comes accuracy; out of chaos, truth.

Pierre le R. du Toit

The hidden people

Ingredients

1 adolescent
$4\frac{1}{2}$ tablespoons co-ordination problems
50g disorganization
1 short-term memory, desiccated
3 tablespoons social awkwardness
50g poor concentration
5 tablespoons original thinking
Special qualities (as many as desired)
75ml undiluted determination

Optional: a spoonful of dyslexia, Attention Deficit/Hyper-activity Disorder or other learning difference; giftedness; a plump juicy talent.

How to prepare

Add co-ordination problems, disorganization, social awkwardness, and desiccated short-term memory to a large mixing bowl. Set aside the concentration and leave to stagnate. Stir determination, originality, and special qualities into bowl and pour in concentration. Add optional ingredients as desired and stir until mixture forms a sticky paste.

Spoon paste into ready-sliced adolescent. Take great care when closing up the body, as the dyspraxic teenager should look like all regular adolescents when you have finished. Bake in an oven hot with social and academic pressure. When adolescent is suitably distressed, remove from oven.

This bittersweet dish can be served with a range of dips and condiments. For a sour bite, opt for bullying, low self-esteem, and lack of awareness. For a lighter and more refreshing flavour, serve with understanding, patience, support, and laughter.

Salaam!

As you're going to spend the next few hundred pages in my company, I'd better tell you a bit about myself and the reason why I am talking to you now. My name is Victoria (Vicky for short) and I'm sixteen years old. I have uncontrollable brown hair with an odd white chunk in it that looks all right when I bother to brush it properly. But using a brush and tying my hair back are difficult to do, so most of the time I resemble a Himalayan yeti. This not-very-graceful-image is enhanced by huge feet that protrude from beneath my jeans like a pair of water-skis, tripping up anyone who passes by! I am also very tall for my age – or I thought I was, until a new girl who obviously has a genetic link with a giraffe moved into my boarding school. When I first met her I thought she was balancing on a pair of stilts.

Her name is Angela and there are many interesting things to say about her. She's a really gifted musician, playing complex pieces at sight even though she's never taken a piano lesson. She also has a talent for languages, a pair of lovestruck stalkers, and an illness called

Chronic Fatigue Syndrome. On some days she can barely move without her walking stick and when she needs to sleep her body shuts down in seconds. This clearly isn't the best problem to have when you've got two fellow boarders following you about, loudly declaring their love for you! She once fell asleep in the computer room and woke to discover them adoringly filming her with a camcorder. Most people's reflex action at this point would be to run for the hills, but Angela didn't even have the option!

We made friends over our shared lack of stair-climbing ability. Angela mountaineers up steep stairs with her walking stick and I flap my arms about like a dying albatross as I follow. We look as if we're performing a slapstick double act, only I don't have her illness. I will explain more about my difference in a moment.

Now that I board at Colditz Castle (not its real name, obviously, but with hulking shaven-headed rugby players, a pair of stalkers and a shifty-looking housemaster wandering about, you could be forgiven for thinking that it was) I only go home to Saudi Arabia for holidays. Five years ago, when I was a sunburnt eleven-year-old splashing in the Red Sea, I would never have imagined that I'd one day end up at boarding school. Boarders follow strict routines and I'm as unpredictable as a sandstorm. Boarders are sociable and hang around in noisy common rooms, and trying to squash me into that kind of environment was like trying to wedge a camel through a keyhole at first. I describe life with the hidden handicap as 'lying diagonally in a parallel universe' – it often feels as if God miswrote the postcode and packed me off to the wrong planet at birth. I have quite an unusual perspective on life (literally, as I have a close working relationship with the floor!) and while this is always a guarantee of colourful originality, it can also feel like a cage.

I used to be obsessed with a series of fantasy books by Sheila McCullough, *Tim and the Hidden People*. Books are escape routes into fabulous other worlds. In the family photo album I always have a book attached to my person like a fifth limb and I often get so wrapped up in the pages that I forget where the story ends and real life begins. I was thirteen when I came to Colditz, and I went everywhere with a novel stuck to my nose. I even ate with a book propped in front of me, with disastrous results, as table manners are not my specialty anyway! The school librarian (I have no trouble socializing with librarians) once told me that there was a lot of staff concern over the fact that I seemed to be hiding from the world. I didn't mean to be antisocial. I just prefer books to human beings because they're easier to get along with – and much better company.

I now know that all this is because of the learning difference that I have. When I was diagnosed with it last year, my thoughts flew immediately to Sheila McCullough's *Tim and the Hidden People*. Hidden people exist. I am one of them. I have dyspraxia.

What dyspraxia is (and what it isn't)

> Dyspraxia is a funny word,
> It's rather hard to say or write,
> But having this dyspraxia,
> I have to say is a fight!
>
> *Matthew, 14*

The autistic spectrum is sometimes compared to an umbrella, with lots of people huddling beneath it in different places. Autism, Asperger Syndrome, Attention Deficit/Hyperactivity Disorder (AD/HD), dyslexia, dyspraxia…the terms stretch on, sometimes overlapping, always remaining vivid and varied. But this umbrella has holes in it and some people are getting soaked whilst others are only drizzled on. I know this because one of my nephews is autistic. What does the world look like from beneath Ben's part of the umbrella? He has a lot of problems but he doesn't seem to realize that he's any different from other kids. Maybe for him it isn't raining at all. For this reason I don't like the umbrella analogy. The writer Jacqui Jackson came up with a better comparison. She imagined the spectrum as a kaleidoscope of intermingling colour with each hue representing a difference. I definitely prefer the concept of a rainbow arching over all of us to the idea of never-ending rain.

Spectrum differences can coexist in the same person. Ben is severely dyslexic and thinks in pictures. If you show him the green ASDA logo he recognizes it at once but if you write it out in ordinary handwriting he can't tell you what it says. He also has difficulty concentrating and was very hyperactive when he was younger. He loves painting and woodwork and he talks mostly through art. This is one area of the school curriculum where he really shines. With the teenage years he's retreated more into his own world, focusing on his fascinations and obsessions, but he can reach out if he wants to and that is the most important thing. Not feeling compelled to speak is not the same as having nothing to say.

The term 'dyspraxia', also known as Developmental Co-ordination Disorder (DCD), comes from two Greek words: *dys* (abnormal) and *praxis* (doing). Clumsiness, lack of balance, and poor depth perception are physical 'symptoms' that the term sums up perfectly, but the meaning of dyspraxia goes way beyond the direct translation of the word. Once I read a health book that sandwiched DCD into one paragraph close to the end. The author wrote that dyspraxia is simply 'the diagnosis *du jour*' and that some children just take longer to catch up on motor development. He closes his book with, 'The world has enough real problems; we don't need to invent new ones'.

Now, calm down and wait until I've finished speaking before you charge off to form lynch mobs! I can't tackle that author's arguments with my usual vim and verve (not without ending up on the wrong end of a libel charge, anyway) but I can answer all the people who think like he does. I am sixteen years old but can't use a tin opener, sit on a stool without falling, pour a drink without spilling, or walk upstairs without hanging onto something. When are my motor skills going to develop? When I'm sixty-two? Blatant ignorance of the facts is another thing that bothers me about the dyspraxia-doesn't-exist lobby. Balance, movement, and hand–eye co-ordination are only the tip of the dyspraxic iceberg. If these were my sole problem areas, I'd be dancing for joy – at least, I would be if I could actually dance without knocking innocent passers-by unconscious.

> You can't 'suffer from' dyspraxia. I wish people didn't say that. Dyspraxia isn't a disease. I don't tell them that they suffer from being normal, do I?
>
> *Joseph, 13*

Stripped down to its skeleton, dyspraxia is 'an impairment or immaturity of the organization of movement' (Colley 2000) but it also plays havoc with the organization of everything else. For a teenager, this isn't just a dry term in the ICD-10 (World Health Organisation 1992). It is the fight to produce readable handwriting and a good essay at the same time. It is the frustration that you feel when you're trying to cross the road, but don't dare to move because you can't judge the speed of oncoming traffic. It is the chaos that whirls through your head when someone asks you to plan ahead. It colours every area of living.

> Anything that requires co-ordination of movement or thought, even a simple thing that many take for granted, causes me difficulties throughout my day. It does become very frustrating, because I know what I want to do but my body sometimes lets me down.
>
> *Matthew, 14*

What DCD is not

> The worst thing about being dyspraxic is the people who call you thick when you know you're not.
>
> *Paul, 13*

Ten years ago dyslexia was not recognized as a problem; it was a label that middle-class parents could buy for their underachieving children. Now history is repeating itself and there is an opinion that DCD is the product of the twentieth century's overactive imagination. If I had a pound coin for every, 'Yeah, right!' and every puzzled, 'But you're meant to be so clever!' and every raised eyebrow that has greeted my explanation of my difference, then I would be a teenage millionaire.

I told you before about the author who thinks that dyspraxia is nothing more than a fashionable label, making it sound as if it carries the same kind of prestige as Miss Sixty or Fcuk. He seemed to think that this fancy Greek word hasn't been around for very long. But the term was actually coined by a doctor in New Zealand in the 1930s – only it didn't catch on. Children continued to be diagnosed with either Minimal Brain Damage or Clumsy Child Syndrome, two very insulting labels that are now fortunately dead. But although the names have changed over time the condition remains the same.

Charlotte Brontë's *Jane Eyre* is a Victorian novel that follows the life of an orphan who is sent to a harsh and impoverished boarding school. (An interesting piece of symbolism there for my housemaster, Mr S!) In the icy winter gardens Jane catches sight of a girl engrossed in a book. Helen Burns isn't interested in gardening or games. She is abrupt with Jane on their first meeting and has no friends of her own age, preferring to be 'absorbed, silent, abstracted from all round her by the companionship of a book…' She spends most of her time in a haze of daydreams ('She looked as if she were thinking of something…not round her or before her. I had heard of daydreams – was she in a daydream now?') but Jane adores her; Helen is intelligent, honest, kind and thoughtful. But despite her abilities Helen is always being cruelly punished and she genuinely believes that she deserves it:

> I am…slatternly; I seldom put, and never keep, things in order; I am careless; I forget rules; I read when I should learn my lessons; I have no method…I cannot *bear* to be subjected to systematic arrangements…

I nearly tumbled out of my seat in shock. Hurriedly reading on, I came to the part where Helen is scolded for having poor posture and is whipped for untidiness. The confused Jane tells her friend, 'It is so easy to be careful'. Helen replies:

> For *you* I have no doubt it is… Your thoughts never seemed to
> wander when Miss Miller explained the lesson…mine continu-
> ally rove away; when I should be listening to Miss Scatcherd
> and collecting all she says with assiduity, often I lose the very
> sound of her voice; I fall into a sort of dream.

Jane is puzzled by her bright but clumsy daydreamer of a friend, for 'at
that moment Helen wore on her arm the "untidy badge"; scarcely an
hour ago I had heard her condemned by Miss Scatcherd to a dinner of
bread and water on the morrow because she had blotted an exercise in
copying it out'.

That last sentence immediately sent me onto the Internet. I found
an article all about Helen ('Fiction's first dyspraxic') and a fascinating
revelation – Helen isn't fully fictional. Charlotte Brontë based Helen
on her own sister Maria, who was too clumsy to sew like a proper
young lady and who certainly couldn't produce elegant Victorian cop-
perplate handwriting. She suffered terribly at school in spite of her
ability. The sadistic Miss Scatcherd is an exact portrait of one of
Maria's educators.

Emily Brontë, author of *Wuthering Heights*, shared some of Maria's
problems: she could not bear to be away from home, was very
awkward around other people, and rarely spoke. Offsetting her quiet-
ness was a stormy temper that burst forth when something happened
to upset her rigid routine. She loved her solitude and spent hours wandering the moors. Autism? Asperger Syndrome? Who can know?

Around the same time, dyslexia was first identified in the person of
a fourteen-year-old lad called Percy. Since those days, dozens of
famous people have been identified as having traits of dyspraxia and
related differences. Samuel Taylor Coleridge was too disorganized to
cope with university and had to join the army – but he couldn't keep
his balance on his horse and was too clumsy to be any good with a
weapon, so he started writing poetry instead. He claimed to feel a
sense of social isolation all his life.

The teachers of the author G.K. Chesterton – 'a slow and awkward
boy' with such a weak short-term memory that he often arrived in a

place and wondered why he was there – once said, 'This boy has a possible career as either an idiot or a genius'.

Albert Einstein couldn't remember his times tables, got lost in his own neighbourhood, was unable to tell left from right, couldn't bear the feel of socks on his skin, and was expelled from school because he couldn't pay attention in class. He was still unable to tie a pair of shoe-laces when he died.

Winston Churchill, Britain's prime minister in the Second World War, is also thought to have shown traits of Developmental Co-ordination Disorder. Generals Patton and Eisenhower showed symptoms of dyslexia. This means that three disabled people kicked Hitler's a...ahem...rear parts, and this really cheers me up – especially when you consider that Hitler thought that there was no room in the world for different minds. This shows that DCD isn't just an excuse born of modern-day hypochondria. It is threaded throughout history, a nameless strangeness.

Explain yourself!

> I'm not stupid, but the amount of times I've been made to feel it, just from a look, is too many to count. I think I would rather be shouted at, because at least I could explain myself then. Mind you, I shouldn't have to explain myself. People should be more tolerant.
>
> *Stuart, 11*

When I got my diagnosis I fizzed out of the assessment room, bursting with relief and wanting to shout to the world, 'Hello, I'm not a freak! I am dyspraxic!' I would definitely have looked extremely weird if I had done this, so it's lucky that I resisted the urge! But since that first outburst of hurray-I'm-dyspraxic excitement, I've learnt to keep quiet. Learning differences are not topics that you can discuss chattily over a Costa.

I noticed this even before I had a name for my problems because of my autistic nephew. One day we were playing in a jungle gym and a little girl asked to join in. When she saw Ben struggling with his poor overloaded senses, she wanted to know if he were a 'schizo' and backed away. The girl's mother shot us a nervous glance and chose a table hidden behind the helter-skelter. Or perhaps her expression was pitying, or even embarrassed. I don't know. I am not good at translating faces. But what I do understand, though, is that people often react to very simple things in stupidly complicated ways.

> When it comes down to it, I could be a lot worse off so I just make do with what I have. I don't want pity or anything like that because there are people a lot worse off than me. There is one thing that I would like, though – understanding from the people around me, especially teachers. I would like the teachers to know why my concentration is poor and it is not because I'm a bad person.
>
> *Shaun, 17*

Why?

At one school I attended, I noticed that whenever our class straggled into the languages block for German, one girl always veered off alone into another building. I didn't dare to ask where she went until one boy muttered, '*Spaz* classes!' as she vanished round the corner.

Many students with special needs are very furtive about their differences. They come and go from their support centres like thieves in the night, hoping that no one will see and no one will know. My friend Emma was always very open about her dyslexia and I try to be that way about my differences, because I'm nearly at the top of the school now and no one will dare to shout, 'Spaz!' at me – and if they try, they will be in for a shock. Unless the secrecy is stripped from special needs, how will people come to understand them? There is an army of terrific students in our support centre (I will let my modesty slip and count myself in) with a mix of different abilities, and it is sad that this wealth of talent is misrepresented by rumour. The only way to change this is to be openly accepting of who you are, although this may seem like a difficult choice to make at times.

Who?

Who you choose to tell about your dyspraxia depends on your specific needs and the stage you're at. Teachers generally have to be told because if they don't know, how can they help? If there is a support department at your school, the Special Educational Needs Co-ordinator (SENCo) will probably speak to the staff for you. If there is no official SENCo then things become stickier. In this situation, bring on the parents – in my experience, teachers take things much more seriously if they hear them from an adult's mouth.

I used to see teachers as untouchables with no lives outside the classroom. They were two-dimensional puppets, existing only to chalk on the blackboard and mark tests. But as you grow older you start to notice that teachers do have personalities. Sadly, there are some who seem to revel in pointing out the problems of people like me and then in feasting on our shame-red faces like mosquitoes after blood. I cannot understand this behaviour and will not try to. If there is no SENCo at your school and you have a teacher who rightfully belongs in some despotic banana republic, you might feel safer keeping knowledge of dyspraxia to yourself. I had one maths teacher who refused to admit that I had any problems other than laziness and insolence. Trying to explain what goes on in my head when I look down at a page of numbers was about as productive as talking to a five-barred gate, and in the end I had to concentrate my efforts on showing her that she was wrong, rather than talking about it.

Occasionally (just occasionally!) you might run into trouble in public and find yourself surrounded by the mayhem that only DCD can cause. However tempting it might be to pin a sign to your back that reads, 'I'M DYSPRAXIC. I CAN'T HELP IT', this isn't a practical solution! When I hold up the queue in shops as I frantically try to sort my money, with the impatient cashier sighing exaggeratedly, I don't give in to the burning desire to evangelize with Dyspraxia Foundation pamphlets. I smile dazzlingly, say a polite, 'Good afternoon' and sail off in a dignified manner (knocking a few things over in the process). Sometimes it's better just to walk away.

Even if you're a born crusader and your goal in life is to raise awareness, remember that talking too much is as bad as talking too little. Can you imagine how you'd feel if, five minutes into a casual conversation, a semi-stranger brought up a really controversial subject and started to declaim their opinions? (If you are anything like me you would probably enjoy it, but I'm told that most people don't!) Even your friends and family might get a bit sick of hearing about dyspraxia whenever you're around. It might be a big deal in your life but most teenagers can't understand.

How?

One of the hardest things about being one of the real-life hidden people is knowing how to explain that you think differently. Teenagers with DCD often have really strong language skills, but when you're frustrated or nervous it gets difficult to package your thoughts in simple, neat sentences. Sometimes I am reluctant to talk about my dyspraxia because I'm scared that my explanation won't come out right.

However, awareness of the hidden handicaps is rising now. If someone is dictating a phone number to you and is getting sharp as your pen stumbles over the numbers ('I said 6945! Look, you've written 655!') then taking a deep breath and politely saying something like, 'I'm a bit dyspraxic and I need you to repeat that more slowly, but I'll get there in a minute' could cause them to completely change their attitude.

Fear of changing attitudes might make you even more nervous about explaining yourself. *If my friends find out that I'm 'different', will I lose them?* If this thought has been swimming around in your head recently, drown it. Your friends have probably noticed your differences already. You can't exactly hide your love affair with the ground, and your dyspraxic quirks are probably what attracted your friends to you in the first place. As people grow older they start to search for originality and they begin to venture out of their penguin-huddles. This makes it much easier to talk about this kind of stuff.

I still wouldn't have told my roommates about DCD if I hadn't had to live with them. I worried over their reaction for days beforehand, like a dog chewing on a sock. Hopefully I have made the process of sharing easier for you. Give your friends this book, show them the passages you want them to read and leave them to it. If you can't explain things yourself, could you ask a teacher to help? Keep in mind that your friends are likely to think that dyspraxia is much more terrible than it really is if they are herded into an office and given a lecture on specific learning differences. Make sure that your teacher can handle the situation sensitively. Some are good at this but others are hopeless, probably because they've never had any practice.

Although it may be hard to make the decision to talk about dyspraxia, most people really do care and they want to help. But if you do have to work or spend time with hurtful people who just don't get it, exploding with anger or deciding not to bother with them isn't possible. The important thing is to make sure that you don't change when you're around these people. You can't control their thoughts and actions but you can control your own. A dose of politeness is a very effective antidote to many cruel comments or awkward situations. Try to be patient with this kind of person because they can't help having tunnel vision.

I sound very considerate, writing that, but when my temper is up it is hotter than the Sahara at midday and it's difficult not to lash out with a barrage of, 'Well, what do you know?' I would like to put these people inside a dyspraxic body just for a day. I have a shrewd suspicion that they would change their minds by nightfall – especially if they were made to participate in a PE lesson and then plough through hours of homework. Add a spaghetti dinner to their day and they would soon surrender!

> When I was at school, it was hard for some people to accept that I had problems because they couldn't see dyspraxia and unfortunately some people are unable to see past the end of their nose...I guess what I'm trying to say is dyspraxia has taught me a lot and one of those things is to NOT be ashamed of it, or try

and ignore it, because it won't go away. I've met all kinds of
people, some understanding, some not, but I can rest assured
that I and the people I care about most have enough intelligence
to understand my disability and that's the most important thing.

Charlotte, 16

CHAPTER 2

The Hidden People at Home

This mess is a place!

Unknown source

I can't spread butter on toast, pour water, or slice bread. Opening bottles? That's always good fun. My arms wave about when I try to run upstairs and I still can't ride a bike. I'm always knocking into furniture and my sisters say it is like having a rhinoceros from the zoo in our house!

Joseph, 13

Déjà vu, anybody?

Home is meant to be a place where you can kick back and relax ('kick' being the operative word) but when I'm there it often resembles a war zone. Here is a summary of a typical relaxing evening. I go into the Colditz kitchen to make a drink, starting with a disagreement with the kettle. The kettle wins. Trying not to shriek, I flail my scalded arm around, knocking over the sugar and punching another boarder in the ribs. I then lose my balance and nearly pitch into the sink, sending cocoa powder cascading onto the floor and causing an anguished cry of, 'Vicky, what are you doing?' as I overturn someone's Instant Noodles. I hope you enjoy this stay in my house.

Soothing the senses

A jumbled jigsaw

Has anyone ever told you to eat your words? For me this old saying has a very literal meaning. When I speak, I can physically taste the words on my tongue. This is connected to a condition called synaesthesia, which is when the five senses blur into one another. Taste and sound are all one with me. I was really shocked when I found out that this isn't normal for everyone. I still find it staggeringly impossible to imagine being any different.

Not every dyspraxic person is a synaesthete, but most of us seem to have different sensory perceptions. This could be to do with the way our brains are wired. Our senses feed us either a strong sharp dose of what's going on around us or a weak, diluted mix of it. I'm very sensitive to noise but have a pain threshold that scrapes the moon. I once walked round with a broken arm for an hour and even tried to join in a game of badminton before I vaguely realized that it was hurting a little. This kind of sensory dysfunction is useful in some respects but very dangerous in others. By the time I finally reached the medical centre my arm wasn't a very attractive sight!

Many of us have strong aversions to certain tastes, textures, sounds, or smells. Itchy wool or lace and the feel of mashed potato or lumpy sauces in my mouth drive my senses mad. People who crowd me get rude and abrupt responses and in busy areas like the Colditz common room I dissolve into a sweaty-faced shaking wreck. Why rugby lads enjoy bashing tables, screaming at each other, and making monkey noises is far beyond my ability to fathom!

When I was younger I had a lot of habits that appeared strange to other people. (OK, OK, I admit it, I still do.) I would curl my hand into a fist and press it hard against the centre of my forehead, or seize one of my wrists and apply as much pressure as I could. I also like to rock back and forth on my knees or stalk up and down in a straight line. The motion is incredibly comforting and I can do it for hours after a difficult day. My roommates find it a bit unnerving so I now have to do it in the corridor. I also carry a pencil everywhere and I flick it obsessively,

annoying everyone very much. I've tried to cure myself of this –
pencil-flicking is impractical when you're washing dishes or having
university interviews – but I just can't. My thoughts are whipped into
an uncontrollable tornado if I don't have HB to hand! Ever since I
began to talk I have called my pencils my 'thinking sticks'.

When I was about eleven years old, I went to Blackpool Pleasure
(hmm, I would debate that) Beach with my half-sister and my two
nephews. At one point we had to pass beneath a rocket ride. My sister
trundled the pram beneath the spinning metal capsules without once
looking up, but I stopped and stared in sickish fear at those whirling
rockets. Crowds of people milled beneath them, their faces going from
sun to shade as the enormous shadows spun overhead, and to me the
sight was terrifyingly surreal. The rockets were so near the ground that
they would surely smash into my head. So, wincing up at the danger, I
fell onto my hands and knees to crawl after my sister. She turned round
to see where I had got to and was at a loss to see me on the floor,
weaving through people's legs. She seized me by the shoulder and
dragged me up. 'What were you *doing* down there?' 'The rockets,' I
mumbled feebly, clamping my eyes shut as she hustled me beneath
them. Miraculously they turned out to be far above my head.

The paediatric neurologist at the hospital was really concerned
about the extreme nature of my perceptual disability, which she said
was something to do with my balance. She sent me to have a special
eye test to check that I didn't have a visual problem. The ophthalmologist could find nothing wrong with my sight. My eyes are in good
working order, but my brain can't read their messages. Logic told me
that those rockets were too high to hit me, yet I still couldn't believe it.
The perceptual distortion was so real. I sometimes stand by a curb for
ages before I muster the courage and confidence to cross the road, as I
can't work out how far away cars are or how fast they're travelling.

Sound sensitivity is my biggest problem and this impacts on my
social ability. I did manage to survive the boarding house Christ-
mas party, an inferno of flashing light that ripped my mind apart. I
shouldn't really admit this, but I was so scared that I clung on to
another girl's hand for dear life! A few years ago I never realized that

most people don't have these sensory adjustment problems and I wondered why they actually *chose* to subject themselves to this torture. The strange thing about this is that I'm partially deaf in one ear. God knows what I would be like if I had full hearing – I might be able to hire my ears out to NASA as satellite dishes.

- Cut all tags out of clothes and don't buy materials that irritate your skin.

- If you dislike the texture of most materials, wear a thin long-sleeved top that you can bear the feel of underneath your other clothes.

- Ask family members not to make the sounds you dislike when you're around. It really messes with your mind.

- If you find it hard to eat new foods because of their textures, try eating just a little at a time. If you can't manage this then pulverize food in the blender, desiccate it, mash it – do whatever you can to change the texture.

- Take a packed lunch to school or college so that you know what textures have gone into your food.

- Do you find brushing your teeth and cutting your nails uncomfortable or even painful? Try an electric toothbrush instead of a manual one and use an emery board instead of nail scissors.

- Have a pair of sunglasses or discreet earplugs on hand ready for when you go out.

- Soft coloured lights and lava lamps are very soothing.

- Surround yourself with textures that you like. I always wear a velour hoodie when I'm in an unfamiliar situation because velvety things make me feel secure.

Unfortunately you can't avoid disorientating and frightening environments forever. Now that I'm a mighty lower sixth-former I sometimes have to patrol the school over lunch, checking that younger pupils aren't in the labs swallowing acid or writing on the toilet mirrors in lipstick. They shout and shriek until I feel that my head is bursting. My sense of smell skyrockets but my vision goes weird: all I can see is a muddle of faces that won't be decoded. The lesson after this onslaught is English, and even though I love that subject I can never concentrate and I jump at the slightest disturbance. My co-ordination and hand-writing seem to get worse too. It's like having a loud and discordant brass band crashing around between your ears.

Sensory integrative dysfunction isn't easy to cope with but I am grateful to it for some things. We pick up on things that others don't, and are able to see ordinary things in startling ways. To me a Hoover is a dragon inhaling. To everyone else it's…a Hoover. This is all creativity is made of.

Sleeping

Many adolescents with dyspraxia find themselves lying awake at some unearthly hour, counting sheep (or possibly something a bit more exciting than woolly-faced ovine animals) and fidgeting restlessly as time creaks by. Propioception is the jaw-breaking term that doctors use to describe the sensations you receive from your joints and muscles when they are being bent or stretched. Sensory integrative dysfunction kicks in here. If you have poor propioception you'll need a heavier quilt to give your body enough feedback. A thick pillow also helps, as does wedging the bed up against a wall. If the weather is hot then turn on an electric fan rather than shedding bedclothes, as falling asleep without nice solid pressure is almost impossible. You might even prefer a sleeping bag. Another strategy is to use a double-sized quilt and tuck the extra material under your mattress, climbing in through the gap at the top.

- A computer on standby or a plug with a red light gleaming is enough to keep you awake.

- Wear a pair of earmuffs – they will block out the slightest sound, and you might like the pressure they give.

- Avoid taking very long naps during the day.

- Don't drink tea, coffee, or carbonated drinks before bed.

- Increase the amount of fresh air and exercise that you get during the day so that you will be physically tired at night.

- Take a warm bath with soothing bath foams mixed in with the water.

- Aromatherapy is a bottled miracle for many dyspraxics. Try calming oils like lavender. Don't choose zesty scents as they will wake you.

- Listen to a favourite piece of soothing music as you are dozing off.

- Imagine something calming, such as clouds sailing softly across a darkening sky, a black sheet of rippling velvet encasing you (my favourite, as I'm obsessed with the texture) or floating on your back on a still lake.

- Try to get yourself into a steady routine – supper, shower, and bed.

- If nothing works, see if your doctor can prescribe some medication.

- Is it really sensory dysfunction that keeps you awake, or are you worrying about something? Many teenagers with learning differences hate school with a poison. Your sleeping patterns might improve if your school life does.

The dyspraxic-friendly house

The most dangerous area for a person with co-ordination problems is the kitchen. My mum is always trying to convince me to learn to cook, but I keep refusing, primarily because I'm very happy with my fingers the way they are and I don't want to turn them into strawberry mousse. But university life and the dreaded tin opener are beckoning, so here goes.

DCD-proofing your kitchen

- Kettle tippers leave your hands free to position the cup.

- Fixed cutting boards are safer than normal ones.

- Electric tin openers don't need much co-ordination.

- Utensils with rounded, rubber grips are easier to hold.

- Special holders fix jars in one place while you open them.

- Mixing bowls and sieves with rests free both your hands.

- A chair with arms means you can sit down if your balance isn't too good. (A good idea if you're working with knives.)

- Don't store glasses and china in high-up cupboards. This is asking for trouble.

- Label all your drawers so you always know where to find things.

- Store sharp knives in a special knife block.

- Have a mini whiteboard in the kitchen where you can scribble down recipes, cooking times, or shopping reminders.

- Use a timer to stop yourself burning food.

- To borrow one of the boarding house matron's favourite mottos – tidy as you go. (I feel like a huge hypocrite, writing that!)

The second big problem that you may experience with food is actually eating it. You have to manipulate cutlery, stay stable on your chair, remember to chew with your mouth closed and try not to knock over cups all at the same time.

It's a daunting list and one that usually turns out to be Mission Impossible, especially when other people at the table are trying to have a conversation with you, or – as is more likely with me – you are reading a book at the same time.

- Use non-slip mats or a damp teacloth to stop plates moving around.

- Buy cutlery with chunky, rounded grips, or customize the forks that you already have with foam tubing. (All hail to the Dyscovery Centre for their set of specially moulded and angled cutlery.)

- Don't overload your plate. The less food there is, the less likely you are to spill.

- Use bowls with lips and plates that have high rims to prevent spillages.

- Avoid easy-to-spill foods like soup.

- Introduce as many different textures as you can cope with to your diet, so you can practise chewing and swallowing neatly.

- Drink from a long, flexible straw if you have a tendency to miss your mouth when you drink.

- Make sure that you are stable before you begin to eat. Keep your back straight and your feet flat on the floor. A chair with arms will give you added security. Your table manners will be better if you don't have to worry about balance.

- Cups and bowls with lids are better if you want to carry a snack up to your room. Handy if you have to sneak food upstairs without giving the game away to prowling boarding house matrons…

Getting organized

I tried many different things to try to get organized but for my first three or four years at secondary school I was in hell… My parents provided a lot of support, especially my mother, who went into school constantly concerning the bullying and her constant nagging proved a hidden blessing at helping me remember things. Still, when I lose things I get such a sense of frustration that it's all I can do not to tear down the house looking for it.

Hannah, 16

'All teenagers are messy! It's nothing to do with dyspraxia!' Groan, groan. I have only one answer for people who come out with this. If you asked a non-dyspraxic teenager to clean up, you might get some growls of protest, but when forced to it, he or she probably could. With dyspraxic people the scenario is entirely different. We truly don't know how to do this. Dyspraxia is a disorder that is very, well, disorderly! The state of my room mirrors the inside of my head, and when my thoughts are in such a wild whirl I stand no chance of organizing my environment.

At Colditz Castle, when I was getting ready to leave for summer parole, one of the matrons walked in on my packing operations. She surveyed the scene with a look of drop-jawed horror on her face, and I must admit that the sight wasn't pretty: a huge mess, with me and a suitcase sitting in the middle of it.

> 'So all this' – unhurried sweep of the hand – 'is going to fit into one little black suitcase, is it, Vicky?'

> 'Er – yes, miss.' (*What am I doing wrong now?*)

> 'Well, in that case, I am going to sit here and watch you pack.'

Now before you start thinking that Colditz really is a prison camp I will hastily explain that Matron is a very kind and capable woman, but trying to organize me is not the best end-of-term relaxant in the world and she was not feeling too happy at the prospect. However, she couldn't possibly have been as unhappy as I was. Faced with such an organizational task, all logical thought had fled my skull.

Lack of organization is one thing I really hate about this problem. You can't string two coherent thoughts together, you feel sickish and flustered and you don't know what to do next, your brain cells have been overheated and you want to cry tears of stress. Do you recognize this?

Elbow grease is the word!

Sometimes I feel like I'd rather do lunchtime duty four days in a row than attempt to tidy the disaster area that is my Colditz cell. But as my special teacher pointed out, if you do a thorough sort-out of your room just once you only have to spend ten minutes per day maintaining it. It's less painful than letting chaos rule although it is hardly what is known as Fun City Arizona.

- Label all your drawers and cupboards so that you know where everything goes. Some people find colour-coding helpful – a blue label for a clothes drawer, a red one for a CD box, etc. Kids with reading difficulties could take photographs of their different possessions and tape a photo to the cupboard or drawer where each object belongs.

- Get yourself into the habit of putting everything back in its allocated place once you've finished with it, even if you're in a rush. Then you won't have to rip the room apart looking for it when you come back.

- Have cups or labelled plastic boxes on your desk to keep pens tidy.

- Don't try to tidy the whole room at once. You'll end up wandering round like a drunken sheep if you do this. Divide it into small, manageable sections: floor space, chest of drawers, wardrobe, desk, etc. Concentrate on one section at a time, and use the sticky labels as cues. Don't just shift mess aimlessly from one area to another.

- You'll probably start feeling like you're running a marathon and be filled with the urge to slump to the floor. After you've tidied each section, take a short break. Eat a biscuit to keep your energy up but don't put off the work.

- Ask someone to watch over you as you tidy. The school librarian always comes to the boarding house to help me when I pack my suitcases at the end of each term, and she stops me from getting frightened or flustered.

- I have a list of instructions ('How to Get Out of This Mess') pinned to the wall of my cell. When there is no one around to direct me, the list becomes my remote controller. The first bullet point says, 'Bracelets belong in the small round box; other jewellery belongs in the wooden box'. It covers all my possessions and all the different areas of my room, and when I feel upset I take a deep breath and glance at the next step to see what I have to do.

- One of the hardest parts about doing this is getting motivated. I have to promise myself an hour in Waterstone's in order to convince myself to tidy up.

Coaxing yourself with treats helps, as does thinking about hygiene. I may be disorganized but I don't want to live in a Petri dish.

> My memory was bad, to say the least. But it has improved vastly and now whenever I lose something I calm down, and think hard about where I might have left it – and I always find it.
>
> *Hannah, 16*

The passive dyspraxics

Now that I have splashed cold water over the inmates of the boarding house, who are in a collective state of shock at the idea of me daring to give organizational tips to anyone, we can continue.

Home is more than a building. You may have more gadgets than James Bond to help you overcome practical difficulties, but they will be as useful as chocolate fireguards when you're dealing with other aspects of your difference. It is always better if you have the help of

your family for this, as they are also touched by dyspraxia. Disability is
never just one person's problem.

> When I was diagnosed with dyspraxia I was actually happy. I
> recognized it as the answer to that question I had pondered
> about for so long – why I was such an outcast. My mother, in an
> attempt to…how can I put this? Not to hinder me…made out
> that I wasn't really dyspraxic. Whenever I used the 'excuse' on
> her she'd say, 'Rubbish!' She was trying to help me get on in life
> without having this 'chip on my shoulder'. So it was left at that
> for a while even though I noticed more and more of the things
> that made me dyspraxic. It wasn't until I took my Year 10 exams
> [age 14–15] and didn't finish them, that that 'chip' became
> noticeable again. I put it down to not working hard enough at
> first, thinking I'd do better come my mocks. But again no matter
> how I rushed, no matter how I tried, I couldn't finish exams in
> history, English, and especially Religious Studies (RS), along
> with other subjects. I kept a record of the subjects I ran out of
> time for and it was at least six; in all the subjects where I had to
> explain what I knew, I kept on leaving incomplete. It was my RS
> teacher who suggested extra time. Eventually I realized that I
> couldn't just 'do my best' or 'try harder' and that I did need
> extra time. But remembering what my mother had said – albeit
> with good intentions – made me feel like it was cheating.
>
> *Hannah, 16*

We aren't the only ones who need to learn to accept DCD. Some
parents have to realize that dyspraxia is not a handicap, but just an
original way of thinking. It is an integral part of the way your children
are and they can't change that, so you may have to adjust their environment to help them fit in.

After seeing their child struggle, most parents are overjoyed to
have a concrete diagnosis and are determined to do everything they
possibly can to make things better. This is a great attitude to have, but
you must team your own thoughts and feelings with your child's for
you to get anywhere. This is his life, after all, and you won't always be
there to do things for him. Teenagers with DCD are often forced to be

overly dependent on their parents because we're like children when it comes to practical skills and personal organization. I think that this subtly encourages parents to see their teenagers as being younger than they really are. I don't like being caged by my disability and so I'm grateful that my parents and the staff at Colditz have found ways for me to be independent. They do this in a very simple way, explaining that I should never be ashamed to ask for help. 'Everyone needs help sometimes,' Mrs S (a Colditz key-keeper) often reminds me. But if I'm concentrating hard on a particular task like writing out a phone number or ironing a blouse, they don't sail in and take over – they keep out unless I say, 'I don't think I can do this. Can you help?' This way I always feel in control of the situation.

This sense of being in control is important to people with dyspraxia, which is probably why we can't always cope in social situations where everything is unpredictable.

> Making friends is very difficult and I can't do it no matter how much I try. No one is cruel to me at school. Most people speak to me when I say hello but apart from that they don't want to know. I don't like talking much and when I do talk it's not about the things they like. One night at Guides I went home in tears. There were too many people in the room and I was too scared to do anything. After that I didn't want to go outside at all. I felt like I hated myself.
>
> *Amy, 14*

When I was a bit younger my mum and dad would often announce, 'So-and-so's got a daughter just your age. She'll be here next week, so you'll have a new friend!' and all I could manage by way of thanks was a glum, 'Great'. Really, how would they have felt if I had kept turning up with a complete stranger in tow and saying beamingly, 'Here, you lot make friends'? Many of us can't cope with big groups or talking to strangers and we prefer to have one or two reliable friends. This is much safer than being a social butterfly and I hope that all parents reading this can understand our point. For teenagers on the severe end of the dyspraxic wavelength, blending in with the crowd isn't even an option. There are too many pitfalls in the way, both practical and social, which I will talk about later on. This does *not* mean that we live in loneliness. It means that we greet the world on our own terms.

Something that parents should always remember is that these problems are not their fault. If your kid is anything like me, he or she might make you feel like you are responsible – I do this when I've had a bad day and I feel about as dynamic as a wet kipper. The only thing that a sensible parent can do at times like these is dive for cover! I try not to take things out on my mum and dad but sometimes, when my body isn't co-operating and my mind feels as though it's been electrocuted, it does get difficult.

I used to feel like a huge disappointment to my mum and dad, especially when I signed up for tennis lessons. They love tennis and I guessed that asking to join a club would really please them. It wasn't an unqualified success. Add a racquet to a spidery tangle of dyspraxic limbs and you don't exactly have the ingredients for a top Wimbledon performance! It didn't matter that my parents kept praising my efforts and reassuring me that I was fine. I convinced myself that they were lying. How could they not be, when their friends' children were playing proper games and I couldn't hit the ball?

Perfectionism and undiagnosed dyspraxia do not mix. In the political satire *Animal Farm* there is a horse called Boxer, whose motto is, 'I must work harder'. This was the spirit that drove me through the first couple of years of secondary school. But Boxer is murdered, and when I hit Year 8 (age 12–13) my work ethic died too. I didn't want to try any more. I was clearly too stupid to do anything, so why should I give a damn? The nagging belief that I could never be quite good enough followed me into the boarding school where I am now, where I finally received the diagnosis that changed it all. I think it helped my parents, too – now they can finally understand why I am the way I am. I can't pretend that my self-esteem immediately inflated like a hot air balloon. That would only happen in a cheesy airport novel. This is life and I still feel like I might fail sometimes. My mum and dad are never anything but encouraging, but when I'm feeling down all I want to do is shout,

'You idiots! Why do you keep being so hopeful about everything? Can't you see I'm useless?'

The point behind this digression is to give other parents an insight into what their child might be thinking. Since I began writing this book, letters and e-mails have flooded in, telling me that I'm definitely not the only person who is too hard on myself – and on unlucky relatives. Perhaps it will do parents some good to learn that they're definitely not the only ones who are used as emotional punch-bags.

- Establish a routine. People with dyspraxia do not cope well with change and we need a set sequence of events to keep us feeling secure. As telling the time may be difficult, the knowledge that the tea table is always laid two hours after school finishes helps us to understand what two hours feel like.

- Ask for your child's opinion before deciding on a course of action such as physiotherapy or extra tuition. For remediation to do any good they have to want to give it a go.

- Don't accuse your child of being deliberately difficult or tell him he 'isn't trying'. Kids with learning differences have to try much harder than their peers to cope with basic tasks. According to Dr Robert Frank in his book *The Secret Life of the Dyslexic Child*, we actually use up to ten per cent more brain power! Praise effort, not output. Try to appreciate how tiring this can be.

- If your son or daughter is having therapy then make sure they set apart a regular time to do their exercises. This way the therapy gets done (even if it is the most boring thing ever) and your child doesn't feel like his time is being wasted.

- Take an interest in their progress at school. If they're struggling, take a look at Chapter 3 'A Survival Guide to School' to see what you can do to help.

- Remember that they may have difficulty with many household jobs. Help them as much as you can by installing some of the gadgets I wrote about earlier.

- Don't be afraid to laugh. Along with lots of patience, a sense of humour is my family's wonder weapon against the difficulties caused by dyspraxia. What is life if you can't sink to the floor and split your (metaphorical) sides occasionally? Pitching headfirst into a supermarket refrigerator and landing on the frozen peas may not seem like an occasion for great mirth and hilarity at first, but I assure you that it does have its funny (but very cold and lumpy!) side.

- Let your children know that you are there for them whenever they need you. Assure them that dyspraxia is nothing to be ashamed of.

'Someone tell me about DCD!'

My name is Clare and my brother Matthew has dyspraxia. I am eleven and live in Milton Keynes. My brother was diagnosed in 2000. It felt strange that now we could pinpoint exactly what the matter was. Even before we knew Matthew had dyspraxia he was jeered at for being small, weak, clumsy. These were just some of the labels given to him.

He was bullied every day. It's hard being bullied but it's even harder seeing someone being bullied. Matt would be chased in the street for the reason that he was 'different'. On one occasion I was walking home later than usual because Matthew had had to talk to his teacher about something. We were halfway home and two boys were waiting for us. They pushed Matt over and one of them sat on him, while the other one punched and kicked him. I had a heavy lunchbox and book in my bag, and quickly I tried to stop them. I saw the bag was no use and (even though I am not a violent person and would never dream of hurting anyone) I kicked the one sitting on Matthew in the back. He grabbed my foot and I keeled over. I told Matt to run, and he and I got up, and ran. I grabbed Matthew's hand because I was the faster runner, and dragged him all the way home. And this was just one occasion on which Matt was attacked in the street. At one point he couldn't leave the house.

All I wanted for him was a normal life. But then, what is 'normal'?

When Matthew was diagnosed with dyspraxia I didn't really know what it was, but Mum gave me a leaflet explaining, so I soon found out. Matthew having dyspraxia made me feel a little relieved that now we all knew what the problem was. It gets annoying sometimes. Occasionally I feel like Matt is getting all the attention, but there's nothing I can do about it. Also I feel Matthew's really lucky because he gets to stay at home as he's home educated now, and also because it seems like he can get away with things that I would be in deep trouble over if I ever did. He doesn't like doing much with me, because he's a boy and he's older than me.

If you are jealous of the attention that a sibling with dyspraxia is getting, my advice would be to ask your mum or dad if you could have some private time with them – for example: going shopping, going to the cinema, or just staying in with them so that you are getting attention too. Alternatively you could arrange to go over to a friend's to get a break from your siblings.

Even though Matthew has got problems I still love him and wouldn't change him for the world.

Clare, 11

When I arrived in Colditz I found myself sharing a room with three girls who were into parties and dancing and cutting out photos of half-naked male models dripping in fake tan. They spent hours each morning straightening their hair, putting on makeup, and – most pointless of all in my opinion – curling their eyelashes. In other words, they were typical teenage girls.

Enter *moi*, centre stage.

Even though they repeatedly assure me that *I* was the weird one, I still have other ideas! I honestly didn't know why my almost-sisters became angry when I announced that the latest hairstyle made girls look like turkeys wearing wigs. I didn't understand why Marie refused to speak to me when I returned a book she had lent me. ('Vicky! It's a book about girls' periods and you gave it back to me right in the middle of the common room! Did you not *see* how many boys were in there?') And I couldn't work out why they got so nettled about my apparent 'untidiness'. Yes, there are a few books and things scattered on the floor, but I really can't see a problem. It's not messy – is it?

Now I think I know why they got a little cross.

Once they came to understand my difficulties, my roommates' reaction was brilliant. At the end of the summer term, when the matrons were allocating rooms for the next year, we asked to stay together.

'We're used to Milly's stresses…'

'…Abby waking everyone up at midnight by scratching her dry skin and blowing her nose…'

'Shut up, Mil! And we've got used to Marie hogging the mirror…'

'…and Vicky's huge mess…'

'…but we like each other really.'

We still had arguments, which normally ended with, 'Vicky, you are such a freak!' from them and a haughty, 'At least my life is not dominated by banalities!' from me. Much of this could have been avoided if I hadn't put my size-nine foot in it with such alarming regularity. Unable to read facial expressions and so tell if one of my roommates was having a bad day, I'd burst in babbling excitedly about a book I had just read and then wonder why I became the target for a snappish, 'Shut up!' To all siblings reading this, your brother or sister probably doesn't mean to drive you crazy. For the sake of your household's sanity, don't rely on your body to show your mood!

- Share some time with your brother or sister. Chat to them about their day. Go shopping with them. Do something that you both enjoy.

- Talk to them about their dyspraxia. How do they feel about it? Try to learn to see DCD from their perspective.

- Stick up for one another if ever you are bullied. This doesn't mean being violent. Encouraging your sibling to tell someone is enough.

- Go to Dyspraxia Foundation support meetings to talk to other people like you.

- You're in a great position to help your brother or sister with social skills. If they embarrass you when you are with your friends, explain why very clearly so that they know not to make the same mistake again – well, not so often anyway! Let them practise making conversation with you. Pay special attention to their body language as they probably won't be able to use it appropriately.

- Take a break sometimes. I know that a person with DCD can be embarrassing sometimes (a big apology to my roommates). Just remember that your sister or brother probably doesn't mean to upset you. They genuinely don't understand what they've done wrong.

Living as a family, working as a team

My family are brilliant, even though I sometimes don't seem to appreciate them. Especially my brother. I give him a hard time and he gives me a hard time too. I don't suppose any family are any different… When I was going through all the hassle at school it affected my brother and sisters too as I frightened them and they didn't like to see me like that.

Stuart, 11

The subheading sounds cheesy but I couldn't think up anything better. It's like those pep talks you get in assemblies – you know, 'There is no "I" in team' and, 'Together Everyone Achieves More'. Mr S has an obsession with these catchy (not) slogans and he's plastered the walls of Colditz with them. You can't even go to the toilet without, 'Don't be afraid of pressure. Pressure is what turns a lump of coal into a diamond!' staring you in the face, which isn't exactly what you want when you're trying to use the loo.

Parents may become confused because they can't fathom their child's emotions. As a little girl I used to cry because I felt like the school leper, but when my mum and dad tried to help me make friends in the neighbourhood I lashed out at their efforts. I didn't really know how I felt myself. At school you're usually discouraged from feeling down – in primary school by the teachers, in secondary school by other kids. It's not cool to cry. Teenagers, dyspraxic or not, aren't always asking for logical solutions. We just need to spill out what we feel without having to worry about consequences. Try to set aside a time when you can ask your child about school and stuff. Let him know that you care and that you are there for him when he needs you. But remember that so-called 'moody' adolescents (huh) like to retreat into their own world at times. I appreciate my own space now because in Colditz Castle I don't get much. People seem to pop up out of the ground right when I want to be by myself, usually accompanied by a ream of homework that they want help with! Luckily I now have my own room, where I can dissolve into books whenever my social legs get tired of propping me up.

My parents were keen to help me overcome the problems I crashed into during the first year at secondary school. In the days before we knew that my difficulties carried a name, Dad was my after-school maths tutor. We would sit at the table for hours, wrangling over long division, while my mum brewed cups of tea and stuck her head through the door to calm me and to snap, 'Don't be angry, Charlie, she's trying her best!'

DAD: But Margaret, I've explained this *six times*! Vicky, listen to me. You keep forgetting to carry the remainders!

ME: I – I don't understand…

DAD: Yes, you do. Come on now. Concentrate!

Dad would begin patiently but he quickly became aggravated as I forgot things within seconds of him telling them to me and continually drifted off into daydreams. If you are a parent with a good working knowledge of dyspraxia, you shouldn't make homework another reason to hate school. Try to teach in a way that your child can understand. He can't modify the way he thinks, so you will have to modify the way you explain. Different minds cannot work in ordinary ways.

CHAPTER 3

A Survival Guide to School

There is something that is much more scarce, something finer far, something rarer than ability. It is the ability to recognise ability.

Elbert Hubbard

Warning! Contents may be hazardous to your health

As the weeks and months passed, the teachers got more irritated with me. Most of the children ignored me or teased me. I only had one or two friends and became more and more of a loner. I spent many of my playtimes outside the head teacher's office having been told off for yet another 'accident'.

When my mum and dad went to parents' evening, they were told I was lazy, clumsy and did not pay attention in class. The things I was good at, such as reading, went unnoticed and people concentrated on the things I was not good at. No matter how hard I tried I could not improve.

Matthew, 14

When I was young my daily routine involved me crying every morning because I didn't want to go. Once I even locked myself into the toilet on purpose and my mum spent ages convincing me to come out. It wasn't just that I hated school, it was that thinking about it, let alone going there, made me feel nauseous and scared. I couldn't understand why my parents made me go somewhere that made me feel stupid and unhappy.

Less than a year later I am very studious and love to learn. I try hard on my college assignments and read loads. I work hard and try to be polite. It seems that school should have been the perfect environment for me, yet it wasn't.

Charlotte, 16

How many of you really enjoy going to school? Most kids are bored halfway to madness in some lessons and don't get on with certain teachers, but for teenagers with learning differences this mild dislike can congeal into a mixture of hatred and dread. I have spoken to dyspraxic adults who remember lying awake on Sunday nights feeling sick to their stomachs because of the week that lay ahead. Even though things are slowly changing for the better, many children with co-ordination disorders feel that they've had more than their fair share of education by the time they reach secondary school.

School has definitely improved for me since I was diagnosed. My teachers used to struggle to understand me: some insisted that I was gifted and behaved 'inappropriately' because I wasn't challenged enough; others pinned the worn-out lazy label on me. There's nothing worse than being called lazy when you know that you are the exact opposite. When I do something as seemingly simple as putting the cap back on my fountain pen, I have to make a conscious effort (aim – slide – twist!) and it's little activities like this that suck away at your mental juices like insidious leeches.

There is a dangerous gap between primary and secondary education and most dyspraxic kids seem to leave one leg on the other side. You go from having one or two teachers who know you well to having one per subject, who at first might not grasp the way your brain likes to work. Buildings are much bigger and are crisscrossed with long disorientating corridors that teem with strangers and senseless babble.

When I lived in Saudi Arabia I was late for nearly every lesson because I got lost on campus. I would spend a big part of my day wandering round and round in the blazing heat, trying to work out which class I had next and where it was located. I would arrive perspiring and hot, my hair hanging limply in front of my face – and it would often turn out to be the wrong lesson anyway. Class sizes were too big and I couldn't put names to faces. I had to take legible notes quickly and write down my homework and hand it in to the right person at the right time and remember my PE kit and look people in the eye when I spoke bring extra notebooks instructions to follow not fall over on stairs concentrate listen carefully too much thoughts in head hurting…and I also had to be more sociable, which isn't easy when you feel as if the space between your ears is clogged with thick porridge.

Sometimes it feels as if the main purpose of secondary school is not to learn, it's to hang about in the toilets putting on makeup and excitedly gossiping about loads of pointless stuff. At least, this is how it is for girls. I don't know about boys. I have never been in their bathroom to find out.

> My first day at secondary school. Dreadful. I couldn't find my classroom all day and arrived late for every single lesson. I got teased and also lost my bag. I also could not tell the time, so I didn't know if I was late or not. I got bullied many times by troublemakers and a few of the teachers were mean because of the way I was. They couldn't understand me.
>
> *Abby, 19*

Choosing a school or college

- Phone the possible schools or colleges and ask what kind of support they offer. If you have severe dyspraxia you might be better off at a school accredited by CreSTed. This is an association that assesses schools and grades their ability to teach students with learning difficulties.

- Go for a trial day during the summer term to see what the school is like. Visit it as often as you need to so you can get used to the layout.

- Talk to pupils who have special needs (on your own if you can) to find out how they feel about the school.

- Talk to your head teacher, support assistant or any other member of staff who knows your difficulties to see what they think.

Get ready to go

- Make sure that your teachers know about your dyspraxia before term starts.

- Write a list of special adaptations you need in lessons – a chair with arms, a Dictaphone, etc. The support system needs to be in place as soon as you arrive.

- Ask for a map of the school, in pictures if necessary, so you can work out where all the classrooms are.

- If you have problems recognizing faces, ask for photos of your teachers so that you can learn who they are before term starts. You can normally find plenty of pictures in school magazines.

- If possible, get hold of a copy of your timetable beforehand and familiarize yourself with your week.

- Ask if the school can find someone to look after you for the first few weeks and help you to settle in.

- Get a good night's sleep.

- Make sure that your clothes are washed and ironed the night before.

- Eat some breakfast – you need the energy, and chewing is calming.

- Wake up half an hour earlier than usual to give yourself more time to shower and dress. It's especially important to look presentable on the first day.

- Don't forget deodorant. You'll sweat more if you are nervous. (Pleasant, I know, but it has to be said!)

- Make sure that you have all the necessary equipment (pens, ink cartridges, etc.) with you. Make a checklist and tick everything off the night before.

- If you have an older brother or sister at the school, ask them to watch out for you.

- Remember that everyone else will be nervous too. You aren't alone.

School supplies

It's hard to find stationery that is friendly to people with co-ordination problems. I don't like ring binder or lever arch files because I can't open them up. At the end of a lesson when you've got twenty seconds to put your work away, write down homework, work out where you are going next, and get out without bumping into anyone, you need stationery that isn't going to bite your fingers off.

- Carry a schoolbag that has Velcro fasteners or large plastic buckles instead of tiny zips. Backpacks are easier to cart around.

- Use box files instead of ring binders.

- Buy plastic button-flap wallets. You can fit loads of them into a box file. Try to get them in different colours and colour co-ordinate your subjects to help with your organization.

- Have a transparent pencil case so you can see at once if there's anything missing. Tape a list of the contents inside the case or, more discreetly, in the back of your folder. Check all the items back into the case at the end of each lesson.

- Correction fluid is messy and difficult to use. Try ink erasers or whiteout tape instead.

- Battery-operated scissors are easier to manipulate than normal ones.

- Have a personal organizer that you actually use – either an electronic one, or a page-per-day diary. Who bothers with school diaries when they give you such a tiny space to write in?

- Use an architect's ruler with a handle to help you position it on the page. Dotting a piece of Blu-Tak on the underside of the ruler at each end also helps to fix it in place. If this doesn't work, try a roller ruler.

- The Dyscovery Centre sells great gadgets for dyspraxic students. If you need compasses that don't have vampire-like tendencies, this is the place to go!

The danger zones

Fun and games?

> All I can remember trying to do in primary school was fit in. But no matter how hard I tried I couldn't do it. At lunchtimes I would sometimes watch the other children play soccer or cricket. Sometimes I was just about to play except no one would want me to. When we played class sports I would always be the last one picked and the side that ended up with me always moaned.
>
> *Shaun, 17*

Games teachers, this is for you. Teenagers with DCD are not being lazy when you catch us hiding in the changing rooms or making up excuses not to participate. (I am a master at this one!) It's all down to fear of the situation that Shaun describes, and the fear stems from the genuine difficulties that we have with your subject – or, to be more precise, the way these difficulties are often handled by teachers and especially classmates.

The first thing you should do is find out which of your pupils is dyspraxic. This may seem glaringly obvious and a waste of ink, but two days after my support teacher had spoken to the PE coach about my problems, the teacher punished me for something my friend Sharon had done. As Sharon is about two feet shorter than me and is Chinese, I don't really know how the coach managed to confuse us!

If you want the group to divide into teams, pick the teams yourself instead of allowing the pupils to do it. The teenager with co-ordination problems is nearly always the last one chosen and the team he joins behaves like a group of martyrs about to be boiled alive. They were the ones unlucky enough to lose the lottery so they get the boy or girl who can't control arms and legs, let alone a football. In reality it is we who have the worst deal – although some people seem to think that I should be overjoyed at the prospect of whacking a lump of concrete around an icy pitch alongside talented squad players, a privilege that doesn't thrill me all that much. I would literally prefer to sit and watch the grass grow.

I know one girl who is allowed to practise ball skills with a friend when her class does PE, and a boy who sees his physiotherapist instead. Could you make arrangements like these for your dyspraxic pupils? No amount of practice will ever make us appear 'normal' on the sports field. If you think this is the defeatist way out, I challenge you to a game of football. Stuff in a pair of earplugs, don a pair of glasses that either magnify the world slightly or make everything appear further away, and try playing with only the hand and foot that you aren't used to. Add a crowd of people who continually scream, 'Come on! Don't just stand there! Get the ball!' and you're having a PE lesson from our perspective. Great fun, isn't it? Even if the other students are very considerate, the feelings of frustrated helplessness don't go away. We know what we need to do, but our bodies don't speak the same language as our brains and the translator is drunk. If the sight of fairground rockets whirling metres above my head once made me cower on the floor, convinced that they were about to crush me, I'm certainly not going to turn into a sportswoman any time soon. It's depth perception, but not as you know it!

Talk to your student to find out a sport he can tolerate. This is likely to be an individual activity such as cross-country running, as things are easier when you no longer feel as if the potential failure of a big group of people is teetering on your shoulders. When you give a lesson in this sport to the class, give the dyspraxic pupil a chance to do well and encourage him as much as you can. Don't devote all your attention to the school team or the county-level players. If you can help one dyspraxic person to feel comfortable on a sports pitch then you have done something amazing, as hitting a rounders ball is akin to climbing the Matterhorn for people like us.

The games lesson horror story begins in the changing rooms. Changing in and out of kit takes ages, especially when you have to wrestle for a sliver of space in a packed cloakroom that is full of echoing noise and distracting smells. I always need to sit on the floor to pull my top over my head and I can't do this if there are crowds of people everywhere. So my support teacher got me special permission to change in the boarding house and the PE staff gave me extra time to get ready. Changing in a different room also put an end to the catcalls about my clumsiness, which helped me to keep much calmer. After a stressful lesson, most DCD kids aren't in a fit state to even speak clearly, let alone take on a group of jeering 'team-mates'. Teachers, please spare us this additional ordeal if you possibly can.

I was also allowed to leave the lesson before PE five minutes early, so I could take all my books and schoolwork to the classroom I would be in after sports. This was because the PE lesson often left me so agitated and flustered that week after week I would forget my belongings, frantically rushing round school in a panicky attempt to trace them. Slicing five minutes off the end of a lesson can stop you from plunging into panic and not being able to think properly for the rest of the morning.

'When going through hell, keep going!'

The man who said that was Winston Churchill, and as he too showed symptoms of dyspraxia, I think it's good advice to take, especially in sports lessons. I hate games so much that I feel like I want to dish out my best excuses for getting out of them, but my sensible attitude to life (and the fact that no one would publish something like that) is stopping me.

No matter whether or not your teachers are understanding enough to make allowances, you must do your level best. Skiving is not the answer. Of course, I *never* do that! (Even the most dyspraxic amongst you should be able to pick up on the sarcasm dripping off that.) I know that none of us is aspiring to join the national rugby team so swimming through a sea of mud after a squashed ball seems like a pretty stupid thing to do. But sport will keep you in good physical shape – although rugby isn't the best example I could name, given the amount of injuries sustained by my school's First Fifteen. One of them got taken off in an ambulance today with hypothermia and winter term wouldn't be winter term without a smattering of broken ankles.

Sometimes I am glad that I have these problems because sport is often treated as a cult. The First Fifteen must have even more severe perceptual difficulties than I do, as they appear to think that the globe is shaped like a rugby ball. I once walked into the Colditz dining room and there was the coach, surrounded by six walking mounds of mud, all of them staring with glazed eyes at the condiment pots. The coach grabbed a pepper pot and went, 'This is the fly-half!' as he grimly whizzed it across the table. 'So we attack!' – butter bowl goes into action – 'And we pass the ball!' – salt pot skitters along, spilling powder everywhere – 'Do you understand the tactics? Right, now we're all going for a run to get fit!'

Why are we the ones who get called weird?

Other co-ordinated conundrums

Appropriately, here at Colditz the Combined Cadet Force is compulsory for students aged fourteen to sixteen. Target practice? I groan at the memory. (For any CCF officials reading this, it is really not advisable to give a dyspraxic cadet a gun!) Once per term, three times per year, eight times in total, I had to go on a field day. We disguised ourselves as trees and were carted off to an assault course, which bristled with signs saying, 'Hazardous – Trained Soldiers Only'. We fifteen-year-olds were issued with bike helmets and sent off to scale ten-foot walls, swing on monkey bars, and balance high above the earth on narrow strips of wood. Is it any wonder that I had to be rescued? On four successive occasions? According to the people in charge this sort of thing is character-building. According to me – and I clearly have more sense – it is tantamount to suicide. Falling into a freezing river in mid-November is not high on my list of priorities!

Teachers, please be wary of putting your students in situations where they're going to experience trouble, unless they feel brave enough to have a go. I went flying and really enjoyed piloting the glider, even though my support teacher was begging me not to go. But my mind was made up and my logic was simple. Even I can't find something to crash into three thousand feet up in the air. Just the occasional high-flying pigeon.

I think the thing that frustrates me most is that I would love to play rugby or go skiing but no one I know will let me do either as they're all convinced I'll damage myself or someone else! This is almost certainly true, but it would be great to have a go!

Adult with dyspraxia

Numbers don't add up

I hate maths. I can never remember the shape of the numbers and my graphs and charts are too messy to read. I never understand the questions, even when the teacher explains them to me six times. They don't make sense.

Paul, 13

I once read an interesting article that traced dyspraxic difficulties with numbers back to primary school. The author argued that children with fine-motor problems can't count on their fingers and this prevents them from succeeding with the basics, ruins their arithmetical skills and fosters a hatred of maths.

A cocktail of short-term memory problems, poor spatial awareness, and an inability to pick up on pattern and sequence means that dyspraxic people usually have a very hard time making sense of mathematics. Students with concentration difficulties can't sift through mounds of irrelevant information just to pull out one answer. Pupils with perceptual problems can't mentally picture shapes and spaces, making topics like geometry nothing more than a meaningless haze. Manipulating a compass that seems to have a deep desire to drink your blood, keeping numbers in neat columns, and remembering all the rules and procedures are all really difficult tasks.

The language of mathematics is an unfathomable mystery. Division signs shimmer into pluses before my eyes and I have not yet grasped the purpose of algebra. Letters are letters and numbers are numbers, and never the twain shall meet. This is meant to be such a logical subject, but as far as I am concerned the words 'maths' and 'logic' don't belong in the same sentence. For example, to solve the equation $n^2 \times n^4$ you would assume that you multiply the two numbers together, wouldn't you? But no, you…add them up. And people wonder why we get confused between + and x signs!

- Use large-squared paper. This makes it easier to set out problems and equations without the numbers jumbling into one another.

- Use a coloured pen to make answers and formulae stand out.

- Ask the teacher to clarify each point several times, using different words. Don't be afraid to keep asking until you understand.

- Instructions are always difficult for a dyspraxic person to follow and in maths lessons they can really trip you up! Teachers, don't go from A to C because B seems so blindingly obvious that it's hardly worth pointing out – it might not be so clear to us. Be precise.

- Repeat problems and equations that you know how to do again and again like a cow chewing cud. Incredibly boring, I know, but it does cement things in your head. If you're having a bad day and your short-term memory is fuzzy, routines come to the rescue.

- Tape lists of mathematical procedures into the back of your exercise book (i.e. the order of operations: **B**rackets, **D**ivision, **M**ultiplication, **A**ddition, **S**ubtraction) so you have something to refer to if your memory fades out. A chart explaining what all the different symbols mean is also useful.

- Buy a bigger compass. If you have a larger surface area to grip you are less likely to stab yourself with the business end.

- Have a calculator with a bigger display screen and larger buttons.

- Use solid shapes when you are answering questions about perimeter and volume, especially if you have poor spatial awareness – holding the shape in your hand is easier than trying to picture it mentally.

- Make numbers and mathematical symbols out of play dough and use them to solve equations. This strategy is great for revision. Things become much clearer if the process is physical rather than only mental.

> I struggled to get through school, especially maths. I wanted to be an engineer and so had to take maths all the way through to university. Well, I struggled and I put in an awful lot of work, especially at university, but I managed it and I am an engineer so it can be done.
>
> *Adult with dyspraxia*

Science lab strife

Co-ordination problems + hydrochloric acid = ...?

When you're perching on a high stool with no back or arms, you may be so busy trying to keep your balance that you can't listen to the teacher. If it's a lecture you are disadvantaged; if it's a set of safety instructions you're in danger, as I know very well – conical flasks have an unfriendly habit of shattering as soon as I get within three feet of them, and when we did our chemistry coursework my partner and I had a huge anomaly on our graph that we couldn't explain. I did suggest writing, 'One of us knocked over the apparatus halfway through the experiment, slopping H_2O everywhere' but the teacher thought this was not scientific enough.

- Stand up if you can't manage to balance on one of those parrot-perches they give you in science labs, or else sit by a wall so that you can brace yourself.

- Try not to move about too much, particularly if other people are carrying chemicals, fire, or glass bottles around.

- Organize experiments before you begin. Ask your teacher for a written list of procedures so you can't forget the instructions.

- Ask someone else to measure out acid or light the Bunsen burner. You could do tasks that don't compromise your fine-motor skills.

- Check that all apparatus is positioned away from the edge of the bench.

- In some schools the teacher may allow you to do a 'virtual experiment' – you type instructions into a computer and watch the experiment unfold on the screen. The same level of scientific knowledge is required, but the risk of deforming yourself is taken away. Unfortunately not all schools have this facility.

Handwriting and hieroglyphics

> My handwriting was always bad, although I learnt to read very quickly. I was good at reading but I didn't like writing because I couldn't write as fast as I thought.
>
> Lucinda, 15

One teacher used to tell me that my writing reminded her of ancient Hebrew manuscripts and that the only people who would have been able to read it were inhabitants of Jerusalem, circa 1000 BC. Luckily she enjoyed translating my Hebrew and marked me on content, not on presentation, even if she did make me stagger through what felt like hundreds of worksheets every night. Now my writing is legible, but each turn and twist of the pen takes up all my concentration.

Isn't it annoying when you are so busy concentrating on the formation of your letters that you lose the thought that you're trying to pin down? It is incredibly difficult to write and think at the same time. What's even worse is when you make a mistake on a sentence that you think is especially good. I always have to start again because I hate it when my writing doesn't do justice to my thoughts.

- Shop for pens that suit you. Wider, heavier pens are easier to control, and triangular-grip pens feel more comfortable in your hand.

- Hold the pen in between your second and third finger – for some reason I find this easier than the traditional grip.

- Some find it easier to write on an angled desktop rather than a flat one. Sloping desktops are lightweight and easy to carry around, and a folder placed sideways on the desk makes a good substitute.

- Use paper with slightly raised lines. This helps you to keep your writing level.

- A brilliant way to practise handwriting is to fill a seed tray with damp sand and inscribe the letters with a stick. (This was a method used by the Ancient Egyptian children when learning their hieroglyphics.)

- Bring a dictaphone or a laptop computer to class.

- Ask a friend to place carbon sheets in his or her notebook. Take the copies when the lesson is over.

- Ask your teacher to hand out photocopied notes rather than making the class write them.

Literacy and language

I'm not being melodramatic when I say that for the first two years of secondary school reading was the one thing that kept me sane. Everything was so strange and puzzling back then, and I would retreat into a book and find instant peace. This gift for words has been with me for a long time – I learnt to read extremely early and I fly through books at speeds that astound other people. Interestingly, many of the purely dyspraxic people I have spoken to have photographic memories for the written word. We drink up books in the way that most people need oxygen. But there is sometimes an overlap between dyspraxia and dyslexia, and people who have this rich combination of differences bubbling in their brains may have big difficulties with literacy.

Couple dyslexia with DCD and you could have a multiple nightmare or a multiple birthday present. It all depends on the attitude you take towards your difficulties and the strategies you use to cope. A blind person can't use her eyes to read so she uses her fingers. In the same way, someone with dyslexia and related problems can use their other senses to help them with spelling and reading.

- Make your own alphabet out of Plasticene or some other soft, pliable material. Use it to spell out words that you have trouble with.

- Jumble up wooden letters, close your eyes, and try to spell words by touch.

- When you're learning a new word, colour it inside your head. Rainbow – the 'r' and the 'a' are red, the 'in' is deep indigo, the 'bow' is bright blue. When you have to spell the word, the colours – hopefully accompanied by their letters – will jump to mind.

- Spell the words out loud, taking one step for each letter. Then repeat, this time taking one step for each syllable.

- Look for patterns in the words. Words that end in a 'shun' sound, for example, are usually spelt -cian. Learning patterns can make it easier to guess the rest of the word.

- Write the word on your desk top with your finger.

- Make a spelling tape for each subject with all the key words that you need for a particular topic – for instance, 'geothermal', 'glacier', 'corrie', 'magma'.

- Make up mnemonics for important words.

- Use a computer with a reliable spellchecker for homework.

Teachers can help students to read by handing out typed sheets of information that are neatly spaced out on creamy paper. White glares right into the reader's eyes, making the letters do gymnastics. The Sans Serif fonts are dyslexia-friendly as they lead the eye on.

There are special antiglare coloured overlays available that you slot over a page of text to help you to read. My friend Emma had a turquoise overlay and I wore a pair of emerald-green glasses to stop numbers somersaulting into one another. These are called Irlen lenses, after the woman who discovered the special properties of colour, and they can also help with co-ordination and concentration.

Unfortunately colour doesn't have magical properties for every-one. Some people can scarcely read at all, yet the world of literature is so brilliant that it's sad to miss out. There is an association called the Talking Book Club that can send you audiotapes through the post, as wading through *Macbeth* isn't a good idea for someone who struggles to process words. Your teachers aren't testing your ability to read per-fectly, so it isn't cheating. Now it's all about understanding the text, forming opinions on it, and getting your intelligence onto paper in a way that is fair to the way you think.

It's easy for someone with severe DCD to be misdiagnosed as having dyslexia or other reading problems. This is because they have trouble controlling their eye movements, so they can't follow a line of text and keep on losing their place. If you fold an index card in half and cut a small oblong out of it, you will be able to hold the window over the text and hide all but one line. This will stop your eyes from drowning in words.

Concentration (or the lack of it)

> Another thing that affects me everywhere is my short concen-tration span. If I have to do schoolwork at home on the computer, I have to be facing a blank wall and have nothing on the desk to distract me. If you read my school reports every teacher every year says things like, 'Shaun needs to focus more on his work,' or, 'Shaun becomes distracted too easily'.
>
> *Shaun, 17*

There is a part of the brain called the thalamus that acts like a filter, picking up on important things that you should pay attention to and shutting out the rest. Most kids are able to subconsciously block out buzzing, rustling, chewing, whispering, pen-scratching, sneezing, flu-orescent flickering, bright colours, foot-tapping, and the gleam of the light on the whiteboard. Now, how on earth do they do that? I have always noticed all these things and I can't imagine not being aware of them. They sidetrack me often, these little pathways that lead into another world entirely, and I spend a lot of time caught up in daydreams.

I feel we are lucky in this way, as there are so many subtle shades of colour and nuances of sound pulsing through this world that other people miss. But it does mean that your concentration span has to cover an awful lot of things. Like a piece of chewing gum, it stretches out until it grows taut and thin. Then the gaping holes start to appear.

- Sit near the front of the class, away from anyone rowdy. This sounds very nerdy but you're above those sorts of names.

- Many people find that clinging onto something, like a pencil, helps them to focus. It sounds strange but for me it is a physical way to direct my thoughts.

- Wear earplugs when doing homework so that noise can't pull you away from the task.

- Take short breaks after each half-hour of study.

- Promise yourself little treats and rewards for remaining focused.

- Don't try to study in an environment that is too noisy or colourful. If your home is full of pets and toddlers then go to a library.

- Make sure that your teachers know that you can't always focus and will sometimes need time out. This is nothing to do with boredom – even if the lesson is really good, I often tune out and wake up five minutes later mentally kicking myself for missing things.

- I concentrate better if I'm following a routine. Ask your teacher to give out copies of the lesson plan to help you to focus.

Memory matters

I can remember nearly every book I have ever read in infinitesimal detail and I'm able to quote huge chunks of text from many of them. My retentive memory for conversations and events that happened years ago is also phenomenal. For a long time I didn't realize that this ability was anything special. I just assumed that because I could do it, everyone could.

My auditory memory is a different thing altogether. When a teacher shoots off a list of instructions I mix them up and end up doing everything backwards. When I was taking GCSE science and I knew we had a practical lesson coming up, I would ask for a list of instructions to memorize before class. The only problem was that if something unexpected happened and a new procedure had to be inserted, I would forget everything that came next. I scramble telephone numbers in my head. I put my French worksheets down and, literally five seconds later, can't remember where they are. I get halfway through a piece of homework and forget the question I'm meant to be answering. In my four years at Colditz Castle I have been the proud owner of seventeen canteen swipe cards. When I sheepishly slink into the catering office, the manager groans, 'Don't say you've lost *another* one!'

In polite terms, this is all rather inconvenient. In fact, it is a huge pain in the posterior.

- Take deep, calming breaths. It is so easy to get impatient and want to scream and snarl and bash a few walls, but the more upset you are the more you will forget.

- Try hard to improve your organizational skills. There are tips on how to do this earlier on in the book. This will help you to remember where various objects are.

- Jot reminders down on Post-It notes and stick them all over the house.

- Carry a mini tape recorder everywhere and use it whenever someone gives you an instruction. Make sure you record times and deadlines.

- Don't be ashamed to ask people to repeat things. I used to be very shy about this, but now I'm ruthless. I carry a notepad in my jacket pocket and I make them write down whatever they want me to do.

Hot fish, cold rice

In the Middle East there is a tasty dish where the rice is cold and sweet but the fish is sizzling hot and laced with strong spices. Disabilities are the cold rice. Giftedness is the hot fish. They both end up in the same mouth.

The frightening thing about being gifted and dyspraxic is that teachers either eat a piece of fish or a forkful of rice, never a mixture of both. They either see you as a clever kid who isn't living up to your potential or as a student who struggles. This only muddles up the pupil even more. People should be very wary of lumping difficulties and talents into distinct categories. Pablo Picasso was dyslexic and had trouble recognizing figures – he saw '7' as an upside-down nose and '3' as a pair of buttocks on its side. A maths teacher might see him as disabled; an art critic would call him a genius. This shows that giftedness, like so many other things, is only a question of personal perception. Many children with DCD have a special flair for one particular subject and some are even multi-talented. Teachers should understand that giftedness can and does coexist with learning difficulties, even if the practical struggles of day-to-day living crowd it out.

At the other extreme, all the publicity that is given to famous dyspraxic people may encourage parents and teachers to expect every DCD child to suddenly burst forth with a wide array of talents. This isn't a practical viewpoint; like most 'regular' people, the majority of us are average in our abilities. Even though thinking of Einstein and Churchill can be comforting and inspiring to many, I have had to sadly reconcile myself to the fact that I'm probably not going to wake up one morning with a brand new way of splitting the atom fermenting inside my head!

Tips for teachers

> My teacher told my mother I was an attention seeker. I moved
> schools. When I went into Juniors I struggled with reading,
> writing, and mathematics. I used to skip reading books, add up
> instead of times, subtract instead of divide, etc. But when I was
> eleven, I was assessed by the educational psychologist and was
> later diagnosed with dyspraxia and dyslexia. From there my
> teachers would help me, support me, praise me for doing things
> right.
>
> *James, 20*

The Dyspraxia Foundation estimates that one in thirty teenagers are
affected by DCD. Even people with all the mathematical ability of a
drainpipe (me) can work out that this means that nearly every teacher
is going to meet one of us at some point. Please take a look at these
strategies so that you can be ready for this happy day! If you wonder
whether it is worth making all this extra effort for the sake of one
pupil, remember that the number of people with dyspraxia is on the
rise – and as the psychologist Madeleine Portwood once remarked,
anyone who thinks that this is simply because we are becoming better
diagnosticians has his head in the sand.

For self-esteem:

- Understand that we have difficulties in certain areas. Telling us
  that we need to improve is about as useful as installing a
  trapdoor in a canoe. Show us how.

- Make sure that we have a guide to show us from class to class
  for at least the first term. We may have trouble finding our way
  long after other students have got their bearings.

- Set up a buddy system to help us break down the social
  blockades.

- Don't draw unnecessary attention to our problems.

- When the class is doing group work, choose the groups
  yourself, placing us with people who are likely to be
  supportive.

- Use positive language. Say things like, 'You got five out of ten right – let's look at the others in a minute' instead of, 'You got half of them wrong!'

- Watch for bullying. It is a sad fact of life (read *Lord of the Flies*) that groups of teenagers have to have someone to victimize, and they usually pick out the people who don't fit their idea of normal.

- Talk to the other kids about learning difficulties, without mentioning any names. It really does help when your classmates realize that some people have to think and work in different ways and that this has nothing to do with their levels of intelligence.

For effective learning:

- Allow us to take two-minute breaks in the middle of double lessons to boost our concentration.

- If you must hand out huge wads of worksheets, staple them all together first and put time planning guidelines on them.

- Let us sit in the corner if we feel that it will help. We can brace ourselves against the wall, making us less likely to fall off our seats. I used to do this until the school gave me a chair with arms.

- Keep us away from both the window and the busy main artery of the classroom, so we aren't distracted by light and movement.

- Use different colours on the whiteboard to make the text easier to follow and understand.

- Don't be sarcastic, or use too many idioms. Tell the pupil to pull her socks up and she may do just that!

- If a dyspraxic student has his hand up, call on him as soon as you can – our learning curve is *now* and we forget things in seconds. (Hear the moans of agreement there?!)

- You might get annoyed when you've patiently explained a topic to us, and ten minutes later we've forgotten it all. Tell us again in different words and remember that although the information is there, sometimes our brains charge an access fee.

- If you rattle out, 'Do the questions on page 64, copy the diagram on page 70, answer questions on page 73 for homework and hand in on Wednesday' we will do the questions on page 46, wonder why there is no diagram to copy on page 73, and forget everything else. Break down instructions into small components and write them down, so our neurones have no chance to scramble them.

- Have a timetable at the front of the room (pictorial if necessary) so we can organize our day and enjoy the sense of routine.

- Have spare pens, rulers, sheets, and other equipment that you can lend out at short notice.

- The help that we receive should be consistent. A few terms of special education will not cure dyspraxia. The nature of the help might have to change, but make sure that the support is always there for us to reach out and grab.

Understanding behaviour:

- Remember that so-called 'bad behaviour' is usually a symptom of a much bigger problem. Does your pupil start being especially disruptive just before PE? Is his memory always worse in the afternoon, when he's had a tiring morning packed with subjects he finds difficult?

- DCD kids often style themselves as class clowns as a way of hiding their difficulties. This may have been successful when they were younger, but in secondary school this tactic may start driving peers away and attracting negative comments. Clowning around is a sign of panic.

- Watch out for panic attacks or angry, tearful outbursts. I used to get so frustrated sometimes that I would cry and rip up my work. Give the student a few quiet minutes outside to calm down if this happens.

- Dyspraxic teenagers might not be very good at working out how to address you. Talking to other teenagers is completely different from talking with teachers, but we don't always pick up on that.

- If you give the student extra lessons, tell them that it isn't a form of punishment. No one behaves like the model pupil when they feel they're being unfairly treated.

- Ask for the parents' help in checking homework and working out the individual education plan.

- Give us advance warning of any routine changes you plan to make – even if you are only going to rearrange the desks – as we may be unsettled by it. We need solid routines to help us cope.

- We aren't saints in halos. I am going to sound like a massive teacher's pet (well, apart from the time I helped to lock our science teacher in the walk-in cupboard) but I will admit…dyspraxic pupils can break rules. Please keep punishment fair and don't ask for lines.

- DCD doesn't switch itself on at nine o'clock and turn itself off at four. It is more than a classroom disability. You may be annoyed with your pupil because he turns up without the right homework or is sleepy in class, but remember that he is struggling against the current outside lessons.

- Some kids are notorious tattle-tales. You might become irritated when that familiar voice pipes up with, 'Pete's forgotten his work!' This is his way of saying, 'You see, it's not just me. Other people get it wrong too'.

    In my secondary school, I was supported, as this school had a good special needs teacher called Mrs L. I was in her class for the first year and she showed me how successful I could be. She helped me in every way. I used to go after school for lessons on writing, spelling, and reading. If my work was wrong, she helped me to correct it.

James, 20

I had a teacher who talked to me about poetry, cracked jokes, and seemed to like me very much – and yet made me sit by myself, at a leper's desk right at the front. She also insisted that I attend extra classes at lunchtimes and erupted like a volcano if I accidentally-on-purpose forgot to go. This seemed outrageously unfair at the time but now I appreciate that she was only urging me on to pass. As well as teaching me about the hippopotamuses of triangles, she showed me that sometimes you have to do things you would rather not try if you want to get anywhere. Please try to appreciate your teachers' efforts, even if they do seem to be inventing new forms of torture every day!

The great escape

> Since I started home education, life for me has changed. I have gained so much more self-belief and self-confidence. I have realized that as a person I am not thick, stupid, or useless. Although I can't do some things too well, because of my dyspraxia, there are many things that I am good at and I focus on them. At home I am given encouragement and support by my family, which has helped me to grow as a person. I don't feel depressed anymore and feel safer than I ever did when I was at school. Yes, I still have dyspraxia but now the difficulties it causes me are much easier to cope with because I have greater opportunity to find ways of overcoming them. The greatest improvement I have made is with writing. I have my own computer and this has given me a new freedom to express myself. At school, I did not have access to a computer and I could not get my thoughts down quickly enough, so the staff and children thought I was ignorant.
>
> *Matthew, 14*

At first I thought that anyone being home educated would have to hire a tutor and get exam papers sent to the home, but surprisingly this isn't true. The child doesn't have to fit into the National Curriculum but can follow an education plan that is moulded to his specific needs. Education Otherwise is a special association that assists students and parents who are home educating and if you are seriously considering this option you should visit their website (see 'Useful Addresses and Websites').

If you want to go to university or get into a good career, you need to work as hard as you would if you were still at school – or harder. Some parents hate the very idea of home education because to them it suggests a failure of a child lolling about on the sofa all day. For a kid who is doing fine in school, this might be true. But for someone who is really struggling with things like organization, routine, bullying, and forgetfulness, studying at home might be the booster jab needed to motivate them. The only flaw that I can see lies with social skills. You can't really learn to interact from books, so if you leave your school are you sure you will be able to cope in the world of work, when you are surrounded by people once again?

Home education, while it won't take away your differences, could stop the belief that you've somehow landed on the wrong planet from taking over your life and this is why it's good. Most of us know that we will probably never go into home education, but the option is there as an emergency parachute. If things ever get unbearable, we know we can jump. One day, hopefully, it won't be necessary. All we need from our schools and colleges is their understanding.

If I hadn't come to Colditz I have no doubt that I would have been fortunate to scrape even one or two GCSEs. Studying here has altered that. But not all dyspraxic people are this lucky. What I find so strange about the education system is that it is supposed to give you knowledge, not stop you from getting hold of it. Yet any word beginning with 'dys' is often misunderstood and not everyone is prepared to find out why we colour outside the lines. Some things will never make sense to me, and this time it's not my brain's fault.

CHAPTER 4

Making the Grade

I never allowed schooling to get in the way of my education.

Mark Twain

Exam hall help

One day the teacher was explaining about the test. I'd heard it all before, and I was finding it difficult to concentrate on what she was saying. I went off into a dream about a computer game I had been playing the night before. Then I had a bright idea. I would incorporate the game into my story. Twenty minutes after the test had begun, I had still not finished my plan. I was gripping my pen really hard and my hand hurt. I was trying really hard to get my thoughts down, I knew I would be in trouble if I didn't get them down on paper in forty minutes. I had a mixture of sweat and tears of frustration pouring down my face. The ideas were going out of my head one by one. Soon, the test was over and I had not finished. Still, I was proud of what I had done. The teacher was not. She told me that if I did not finish in the proper test I would fail. I was disappointed because I wanted so much to show what I was made of.

Matthew, 14

If I could plug a printer into my brain I would prove to everyone that I'm not stupid.

Paul, 13

Up until my diagnosis exams were a nightmare. Forcing my intelligence into handwriting, organizing my thoughts, staying focused, and worst of all, trying to get through a maths paper without bursting into tears or getting so frustrated that I wanted to rip the thing into shreds, were nearly impossible. I failed several exams because I couldn't complete the papers. When I sat down at a desk in the exam hall my head felt like a big traffic tunnel packed with cars. And even when the tunnel was full the cars still kept coming and coming until I felt my brain was going to explode from having too many thoughts in it and I couldn't spill them out quickly enough.

Yet kids with dyspraxia are intellectually equal to their peers. I am extremely good at English and other language-based subjects, but my spiky letters and infuriatingly slow writing speed made sure that no examiner ever realised it. 'Vicky must work on her exam technique,' my school reports deplored. 'Her grades do not match her ability'; 'Vicky needs to develop time management skills'; 'Her history test mark was surprisingly low'.

Then I had my assessment and it all changed. Now I can sit down in front of a test paper knowing that laptop, extra time and rest breaks will carry me through. I don't have to fight my way through the questions any more – unless I haven't revised properly, which happens more frequently than I'd like to admit!

Things improved at senior school; as well as extra time I was given a computer to do my exams on and a laptop to use in most lessons. The other pupils never bullied me or anything but some of them made it quite clear that they didn't like the 'very loud and annoying' noise of the laptop (which was very ironic because they were the people who made the most noise in class anyway) and they thought it wasn't fair that 'she gets to use a laptop'.

I didn't like to be seen as 'different'. I didn't want to draw attention to myself. I just wanted to be invisible. So often I'd 'forget' my laptop or it 'wouldn't print out'. Actually there were a lot of problems with it but they could have been sorted. Looking back it's a shame I did that. If I'd have used my laptop all the time people would probably have got used to it and it was only a small minority that it 'disturbed' anyway.

Charlotte, 16

Two reasons that stop students with learning difficulties from accepting special help is fear that universities or employers will discriminate against them, or worry that such concessions will just make the situation worse. For some kids, especially those with concentration difficulties, extra time only stretches out the agony. But it should be remembered that there's such a lot of special assistance available that there is a concession to fit every learning quirk. If extra time isn't right for you, the psychologists will find something that is. It is their job to work out ways for you to show your true ability.

Anyone who refused to accept a student or employee because of their DCD would find themselves being rushed into a court of law under the Disability Discrimination Act – and thanks to the work of organizations such as the Dyslexia Institute and the Dyspraxia Foundation, many organizations are now realizing that a different way of thinking can be an asset. If you take concessions in exams no one will ever know. Your certificates don't have DYSPRAXIC stamped across them in giant red capitals. This is because examiners realize that asking you to go into an unfamiliar room that might be full of distractions and think in the same way and at the same speed as students is like asking a regular candidate to do the exam in the dark.

Steps to better study skills

I did my GCSEs last year and I had 25 per cent extra time. I found it all incredibly difficult but I was determined to work hard and do my best so for three months I just shut myself off from the world and studied with all my might. It was hard to revise because writing stuff out made my hand ache and nothing was going in because I was concentrating on the writing, and I am useless at art so 'fun' spider diagrams were hard too, but I managed. I also found other ways to revise like typing things, highlighting key words, making tapes and listening to them, getting people to test me verbally and writing key words and, using Post-It notes, sticking them on the walls.

Charlotte, 16

Here is a mixed bag of tricks and techniques that you can use to enhance your revision. Not all of them will suit you, but take a good look at each and try out the ones you think look promising. I know you must be rushing to get to the dating chapter but time spent here is time well spent! Here are some things that you will need:

- A positive outlook. You can do this. Remember that no one can make you learn – you have to want to do this for yourself.

- Plenty of sleep. For your brain to function properly, it needs to be well rested. As a result of the extra effort we have to put in we often end up extra tired.

- A revision timetable. Draw up a chart of your day and decide on how much time you're going to allocate to your study. Work out what proportion of time you will devote to each subject and stick to your decisions.

- A bigger weekly timetable to help you plan long-term study goals.

- Four document trays to store your work in – one labelled 'to be done now', one labelled 'tomorrow', one labelled 'this week', and one labelled 'this month'. Check the trays every day to help you sort out and remember all your assignments.

- A workplace free of distractions. This doesn't mean it has to be clinically silent. It has to be comfortable enough for you to want to spend time there.

- A good stock of stationery. Make sure you have two of everything, so if you lose your pen at school you know there's a spare waiting in your desk-tidy at home. ('Desk-tidy' = euphemism for 'fathoms deep under the bed'.)

- A library card. If you are going to do well in exams, you need access to outside resources.

- A set of index cards on which to note down important facts.

- Post-It notes. Jot assignments down on these and stick them to your desk, throwing them out when the work is done. If writing on such a small surface is a problem, use colour coding. A blank pink Post-It means you have history homework, a blank orange Post-It means you have German, and so on.

- A planner in which to note down assignments and deadlines. Keep this ready during class – if you have to fiddle with zips and clasps on a schoolbag just to fish it out, you'll give up keeping a proper record. A homework checklist stuck in the back of each subject exercise book might be better.

- You may need a lot of help with your organizational skills. Is there someone at your school whom you could phone each night to check that you have the right homework titles and deadlines?

- Keep all your paperwork in box files. Tape a list of the file's contents (French verb tables, grammar notes, essays on French culture...) to the inside flap of each folder.

- Pinpoint the time of day when you're at your best. Many of us find that the level of our difficulties varies from day to day and even from morning to afternoon. If you know that your problems are napping in the mornings, get your study done then.

- If you're having a particularly bad day with a subject, do as much work as you can, move onto something else for a while and then come back to the problem zone. Everything is more difficult if you're panicky.

Revision techniques

- If you're happy to delve into books, read widely around each subject. Make a list of key topics that you need to revise and choose a good selection of relevant books. Avoid treating revision guides as your Bibles. They are knowledge supplements, not knowledge suppliers.

- You could watch programmes such as GCSE Bitesize, get hold of CD-ROMS, and surf the Internet for study sites, although there are none specially for people with learning difficulties. Are there any web wizards reading this who are up to making one?

- Write down on index cards – or ask someone else to do the actual writing for you – key facts for each subject. Don't overload each card with information. Then highlight key words in colours that appeal to you. For some reason I associate the colour purple with psychology, so all the names of eminent psychologists that I have to remember are written out in purple. Carry a set of cards everywhere you go and glance through them whenever you can.

- Record your work on tape and play it back to yourself. For GCSE Latin we had to learn a huge chunk of the *Aeneid* off by heart. I recited it into a tape recorder, played it incessantly for the next two weeks (narrowly avoiding getting murdered by my roommates) and on the day of the exam…word perfect.

- Mind-mapping is useful if you're trying to organize your thoughts or plan an essay or a project. Make the maps large and colourful and don't crowd too much information onto each page. Techniques like this normally get your brain juices flowing again and unlock ideas.

- For some subjects I revised by writing stories about topics we had covered. It's much easier to produce an exam essay on the causes of the First World War if you've spent fifteen minutes pretending to be Franz Ferdinand's assassin scribbling in his diary as he languishes in prison. This technique might work if you enjoy being creative. Revision doesn't have to be drier than dog biscuits.

- Get together with a group of friends and give each other lectures on a particular subject. Swap notes and work through past papers together. Don't do this too often as 'study session' might just become another word for 'party'.

- Move beyond the classroom. Go to see that play you're studying. Spend a couple of hours in a science museum. Visits that break up your usual study routine will superglue things to your brain cells.

Judgement Day

- The applications for GCSE and A-Level exam concessions have to go to the exam board several weeks before the exams begin. Go to your school or college's Exam Officer, show them your assessment report, and ask them to apply for the prescribed concessions on your behalf. If you don't get this done in time you won't be given any dispensation in the exam hall.

- Make sure you know what is expected from you in each exam. Will it be multiple choice or is it an essay test? Ask a teacher to write down the requirements weeks before the exam, so you can try out past papers.

- When you get your timetable, make several photocopies and keep one in your schoolbag, one with you, one in your bedroom, and one stuck somewhere noticeable like the fridge. If you're taking public exams, copy your candidate number onto each timetable – this is information that you don't want to lose.

- Draw up a list of equipment you will need for each exam, for example, MATHS – ruler, pen, ink cartridges, spare pen, calculator, pencil, sharpener, rubber, crayons, compass, protractor. Tick the items into your bag the night before the exam.

- If you wear Irlen lenses make sure that you have them with you. Keep a transparency in your colour in your schoolbag just in case.

In the exam hall

- Arrive at the exam hall at least half an hour before the exam is scheduled to begin. If you're taking an exam at a strange place (if you're at university this might happen) you should familiarize yourself with the area several days before. Make as many visits as you need to fix the location in your head, and check that you know train times and bus numbers. Allow lots of time for late trains.

- Before you walk into the exam hall, take some deep breaths. Ignore all the people screaming, 'I've barely revised – I only did six hours per night!'

- When they say, 'It's 9:07, you have two hours, start now,' in a voice like a death knell, read through your paper calmly. If there are pages or questions missing in the script, put up your hand and ask for help.

- Read questions several times to make sure you understand them.

- If you can't plan things very well mentally, spend five minutes on a box chart or bullet pointed plan to get your ideas flowing around the question. Show this outline if you don't manage to complete it.

- Look at the marks allocated for each question. Don't spend twenty minutes on a question carrying five marks, leaving just ten minutes for an essay.

- If your handwriting is difficult to read then write on every other line to make things clearer for the examiner and easier for you.

- Leave the questions you find difficult and come back to them later, once you have upped your confidence by working on the ones that you can do.

- You sometimes have to use treasury tags to fasten extra pages to your main script. If this happens, attract an invigilator's attention quickly and ask them to do it for you, otherwise parts of your script will be lost.

After the exam there always seem to be crowds of students performing a post mortem on the paper. Everyone will be crying out what they put and convincing you that your answers were wrong. Don't get tangled up in the hype. Find a quiet corner, relax for an hour with a good book or a computer game, and then focus your thoughts on the next exam.

Remember to look at your grades in proportion to the level of difficulty you have with that subject. I got a C in maths and scored within the top five students nationally for my GCSE English, out of nearly half a million candidates. But the maths grade was the better of the two because of all the extra effort I had had to make. I sat through two hours of special education each week – numbing both my brain and my backside – and I asked a friend to sacrifice some of his study leave to teach me more. I had never passed a maths exam in my life and after I had finished that awful paper I was convinced that I would be crawling through mires of simultaneous equations forever. On Results Day that little slip from the exam board Edexcel was the first certificate I looked at, and the letter C has never been so beautiful. The same went for my science. After my little mishaps with the coursework apparatus I was thankful for any grade. Even the bill for broken conical flasks faded into insignificance beside it!

CHAPTER 5

Crossing the Chasm

When you can no longer dwell in the solitude of your heart you live in your lips, and sound is a diversion and a pastime...In much of your talking, thinking is half-murdered.

Kahlil Gibran, The Prophet

The nameless strangeness

It was discovered that I had dyspraxia fairly late, in my first year of secondary school. Of course I had always known there was something wrong with me, that was why I had no friends, I reasoned. I had to move schools partly because of that, and at my new school it was worse.

I remember making up games to play in the playground alone, hopping on tree stumps or leaping over shadows. Fortunately my overactive imagination provided all the entertainment I needed. I was very sensitive, especially about being left out. Every time I sat alone or was left without a partner in sports the tears would well up in my eyes. I never regarded myself as being unduly bad at sport, just unfit, lazy. But I did, and still do, envy my brother who is 'normal' and four years younger than I.

My social life can't ever compete with Daniel's. As I type this he is going out with two friends to the cinema and he's still grumpy because he phoned up over twenty other friends and they couldn't come too!

Hannah, 16

Living with the hidden handicap can make you feel like a penguin in the middle of the Saudi Arabian desert. Completely out of place.

I have heard it said that the main difference between adolescents with autism and adolescents with dyspraxia is that autistic kids are quite happy to be loners. Dyspraxic people want to join in but they don't have the ability. I disagree. Anyone with a personality has the ability to socialize if they want to, and many individuals with DCD find it easy to empathize with others and are very caring. But even though you have your qualities you might have problems knowing how and when to show them.

I am told that I'm a good storyteller with a vivid imagination. The only trouble with this is that I am what my dad calls 'prone to exaggeration' and this can precipitate me into one heck of a mess. The dividing line between fantasy and reality is blurry, and I can't always differentiate between stories I've read, stories I've made up, and what has actually happened. Another dyspraxic quality that can get us into difficulty is unflinching honesty. One of my roommates once asked me, 'Is my eye makeup OK?' and I said, 'No, you look like a panda'. I thought she wanted to know how she looked before she left the room. Judging by what happened next, apparently not!

There are three main anomalies that make us stand out from the crowd. The first is physical. When I'm talking to people I either stand several feet away from them, as if they have a contagious disease, or I end up treading on their toes. I can't judge whether I'm too close to someone or too far away unless they tell me. I also have a problem with eye contact. I wasn't aware that I was doing anything wrong until I overheard a teacher saying, 'I'm uncomfortable talking to Vicky, she won't look you in the eye'.

Eyeballing someone like Kaa the snake makes me nervous because I feel as if the person can see right into my thoughts, so if they want me to look at them I focus on their nose instead. This guards against the inevitable barrage of, 'Are you listening? Look at me when I speak to you!' Teachers are definitely the worst culprits for this. I once ran into trouble at primary school for replying, 'Well, I don't listen with my eyes. I listen with my ears'.

If you don't make eye contact then people might think you're bored with them – and they could be right, as your interests probably don't come from the standard jelly mould. For example, lads are expected to treat football pitches as holy ground, but most dyspraxic boys can't summon up any interest in kicking a lump of leather about. So they are unable to join in conversations that are saturated in fascinating talk of sport.

Lost in translation

Language is another area where we are unusual. You might be unable to translate sarcasm. (Practise on the above paragraph!) You might use words that make you sound old for your age and intimidate other people, or struggle to understand the way other kids talk. The ever-changing dictionary of slang always has me confused. When I was a bit younger my manner of speech used to provoke angry outbursts from classmates, who mistakenly thought that I was choosing ostentatious words just to show off. It took me a long time to realize that other children didn't share either my linguistic fascination or my vocabulary. I now try hard to be careful when talking to people I don't know. This is why I have dotted this book with words that I wouldn't ordinarily use ('kids', for example; that one annoys me – people are not goats). I don't know whether I have succeeded in this, as my idiolect usually stubbornly refuses to metamorphose.

I garner my linguistic ability from books, not from television or social chitchat, so I have no idea how to pronounce many of the words that I discover. This isn't a problem most of the time, as hardly anyone has a clue about what I'm on about anyway. But occasionally I run into someone who not only has a word bank to match my own but who also knows how to pronounce everything. I get a lot of friendly teasing because of my stumbling speech. (Shut up, Jamie, I can hear you sniggering from forty miles away!)

Some of us also take language very literally and can't understand idiomatic phrases like 'he has a bee in his bonnet' or metaphors such as 'she kicked the bucket years ago'. Our style of speech can also cause problems – you don't talk to your teacher in the same way that you chat to a friend, but many of us find it really hard to tell the difference. How many of you have been accused of being rude when your intentions were far from cheeky? It makes me feel (and this is going to sound cowardly) very afraid when people misinterpret my meanings, as if I have no control over the situation. I believe that your personality colours your speech, so changing how I speak is like changing who I am. Maybe other kids can do this without any trouble, but I lose something of myself whenever I try. I am me and I can't really be anyone else. Is this a handicap?

If you close your eyes during a conversation and focus on the sound of the words it's like listening to a concert. People make their voices go deep or squeaky in the same way that a violin maestro coaxes different notes out of the instrument. They can apparently change the entire meaning of what they say by doing this. This could be why people so often misinterpret me, as I can't always control the volume, pitch, and tone of my voice. A lot of dyspraxic people find this hard and we end up being accused of saying things we never thought of. If I could, I'd lunge at the phrase, 'You didn't say it, but you implied it!' with a racquet. With me, the meaning is always within the words. Taking drama lessons has helped me to get better at picking up on other people's tone of voice and similar stuff, but I still find it infuriatingly difficult to tell when someone is being sarcastic.

There is another type of 'language' used by teenagers that I refuse to acknowledge as a legitimate mode of expression. We have words to communicate with, so what's the point of eyebrows? Unfortunately, it's estimated that around 75 per cent of 'conversation' is non-verbal (though how they came up with that figure I have no idea) so you have to use body language if you want to understand and be understood. Translating someone's face is like trying to make sense of Mandarin Chinese. When you are busy making sure that you are standing in the right place and looking at the other person and making interested noises and doing a hundred and one other things that require much thought and concentration, you don't really have time to notice faces.

Meet the Martian

Finally, there are emotional differences swirling around in our heads as well. How many of you have been called naïve? How many of you frequently get told that you act like you live on another planet? That would be all of us, I expect! I spent much of yesterday lunchtime unable to work out why everyone was in hysterics over a roll of masking tape emblazoned with the logo 'Gaylord' in crimson capitals.

Even though the joke was obvious to all the others in the room, it had to be explained to me in clearer terms. What is obvious to a non-dyspraxic adolescent is often totally mystifying to the teenager with DCD, and vice versa. We notice a lot of things that other people are oblivious to.

In Saudi Arabia I rarely mixed with other English children. My friends were all foreigners who had grown up in cultures so different to my own that they accepted everything I did as typical English behaviour. Maybe in her country they spill food everywhere as a compliment to the chef? But five days a week I had to attend British international schools, where my obvious difficulties made me feel very weak and awkward. So many dyspraxic children grow up thinking they're weird and getting steadily more upset because they can't seem to make friends. I'm guessing that more than one person reading this has desperately wished that there were some kind of excuse for standing out, an excuse that everyone would just accept. I know I used to. Since then I have realized that we don't need one.

I have also realized that you don't need to have enough friends to fill a football stadium in order to be happy. Some children feel like they're missing out because they are often alone. Others are loners by choice. Even though I now have a small group of friends who are very valuable to me, I will freely admit that my books come first. When I'm in Saudi Arabia my favourite thing is sitting alone and silent on the steps of our villa, staring up at the evening sky as the sun goes down and the stars slowly fan out across the heavens. There are some things in life that cannot be shared.

Strengthening your social skills

Vive la difference!

The problem with discussing social skills in the way that we are doing now is that it tempts a lot of us to think of ourselves as pincushions with difficulties stuck all over us. This is a horrifically prejudiced viewpoint that encourages kids who are different to see themselves as somehow inferior to everyone else. Maybe you need to alter your behaviour a little, but you should never change your personality just for the sake of fitting in. If you do this you won't be able to stand your own company. You should also realize that no matter how much you might want to be in step with the world, you will go through life dancing to a different drum. This is no bad thing – just read Digby Wolfe's poem *Here's to Kids who are Different* and you'll see what I mean.

- Be yourself. I know this isn't a sparkling gem of originality. How can you 'just be yourself' when others don't like the person you are? You must realize that you probably aren't behaving like your real self when you're in situations that make you feel vulnerable or weird. Secondly, you need to understand that you aren't a freak or a spastic or whatever ignorant names you may have been called. Be a better friend to yourself before trying to reach out to others.

- Don't judge. I have a nasty tendency to dislike rugby players because in my school they get away with murder. Well, not exactly, but they do get away with leaving bowls caked in scrambled egg in the kitchen for other unfortunates to clean up, all because they have a talent for 'messing with balls', as the librarian puts it.

- If you want to make more friends, start small. Begin with smiles and hellos as you pass people. If a group of people appears to be having an open conversation (when everyone is comparing weekends, etc.) screw up the courage to join in.

- Meet each new person on individual terms. Don't make generalizations based on your knowledge of 'similar' people. This just leads to stereotypes, and this is wrong – even when the stereotype is positive. I used to assume that everyone reads as quickly as I do and has a passionate (if dormant) interest in literature that is begging to be woken up…but it transpires they do not!

- You don't have to befriend people your own age and no one else. Many adolescents with DCD prefer to mix with adults or with younger children rather than other teenagers, as they are more accepting. There is nothing wrong with this. One of my closest friends is a seventy-eight-year-old Holocaust survivor.

Appearance

- Make sure that your clothes are fresh and that your hair, skin, and teeth are all clean. Carry face wipes and a comb with you to school. If you're anything like me, you may come unravelled during the day!

'Don't sweat the small talk!'

> I get confused when people talk to me and I don't understand what they are trying to say. Sometimes I think I have understood when I haven't and this causes problems for me, especially at school.
>
> *Philip, 15*

'Small talk' involves babbling on about nothing in particular. Here is an example:

> 'You so like him.'
>
> 'I so do not!'
>
> 'You SO do.'
>
> 'I SO do not.'

This is a transcription of a not very illuminating dialogue between two fifteen-year-old girls that I took down in the Colditz computer room the other day. Can you see a point to that little exchange? Well, neither can I. But if you want to be more sociable you should involve yourself in these chats as often as you can bear them. This is called 'the art of compromise'.

Pointers for politeness

Even if the people around you wouldn't know what manners were if they jumped up and bit them on the nose, set yourself some standards and don't be afraid to live up to them. It has to be admitted that politeness doesn't always guarantee you friends, but it will guarantee you self-respect, which is much more important.

- Know that there are times when it isn't appropriate to let your anger or excitement loose. You may need to work on your self-control.

- Don't use bad language. Anyone with a vocabulary and an ounce of creativity shouldn't need it, and sentences like, 'I am catching the !*@/!*% bus tonight,' don't make any sense. I can't stand such flagrant mutilation of the English language. Other teenagers may get away with it but you will probably end up offending someone, so don't take the risk.

- Don't ever tell sexist, racist, or dirty jokes.

- If you get hold of a fact that you find interesting ('The toucan's beak is longer than its body!') or a juicy bit of gossip ('Ken cheated on Linda with Jess!') don't rush around telling everyone, or you will be seen as either a know-it-all or a stirrer of *la merde*.

- Do not tell lies – unless someone asks you if they look fat or wonders if their eye makeup is horrible. Then be economical with the truth!

- Be kind and offer help when you can see that someone needs it. Simple things, like holding the door open with a smile, create a good impression.

- If you have very strong opinions, don't argue with other people all the time and try to force them to see your point of view. It is always good to have sound principles and you should never allow yourself to be pressured into something you don't want to do, but others don't need to constantly hear about your beliefs.

- Think before you speak! Here is an example of what can happen if you aren't careful:

(Scene: a group of students chatting in a classroom, waiting for the teacher to come. One girl is sitting alone reading a book. Suddenly she raises her head.)

VICTORIA: Are you talking about the senior prefect applications?

LEANNE: Where have you been, Victoria? We've been talking about those for ages!

VICTORIA: (*politely*) I'm sorry. I don't always pay attention to everything you say.

(She is now told that this is not a good answer.)

- People like to hold private conversations. If you walk in on a secretive group and they stop talking immediately, don't automatically think that they were discussing you. Respect their privacy and leave quietly.

- Those of us with DCD sometimes have a hard time with the concept of 'secret'. If you're unsure whether a friend wants you to keep something private, ask. Loose lips sink ships!

- Get a parent or relative to help you with conversational skills. Work with them on your body language and acceptable social distances. If you stand too close to a member of the opposite sex, everyone decides that you fancy them, and if you stand too close to someone of your own sex, people call you gay. You should always stand at least an arm's length away from people when standing and an elbow's width when sitting...only I can't gauge this without sticking my arm out like a Nazi on parade, so I'm in trouble.

- If the topic of conversation moves on to something else, don't keep trying to bring it back to the original subject.

- Don't be too persistent with a wish or request. A lot of us have a tendency to do this. I think it's because we're unable to understand what it's like to have even an average short-term memory, so we think that everyone needs to hear instructions several times in order to recall them. If they've heard it twice they've got the picture!

- Don't hog the conversation or interrupt other people. Ask someone who knows you well to tell you when you've gone on for too long.

- It is polite to talk about the other person's interests more than your own.

- If you want to do this, you could arm yourself with a few topics that you know the other kids at school will be talking about – the latest cinema release, football scores, a TV series, lip gloss – so you will have something to chat about. I would never deliberately instigate a conversation about any of these things because they would bore me halfway to rigor mortis, but if you desperately want to fit in more this is a tip you could try.

- Think of eye contact as punctuation, to be used at the beginning of a sentence (capital letter) at the end of a sentence (full stop) and wherever you want to put special emphasis.

I know that not all teenagers rigidly follow these rules. In fact, from what I've seen, most of them do not. But you are different anyway, you have other problems and worries to contend with, so you can't abide by someone else's rulebook.

As for stuff like not interrupting people or barging in on conversations, I have to admit that this is something I still find very hard and probably always will. My short-term memory isn't great so I have to blurt out my thoughts fast in case I forget them. There is a gap between listening and understanding, so I hate it when people ask question after question and force me to think quickly. My thoughts get garbled on the way to my mouth and come out differently from how they sound in my head. This is why I love talking to the few people who seem to instinctively understand that I need time and patience. There is really only so much about ourselves that we can realistically change. If we're prepared to try, I reckon that other people should be prepared to accept that we might not always be successful.

Translating body language

The best guide to body language and facial expression that I know of is the Collins Gem pocketbook (*Guide to Body Language and Facial Expression*). You obviously don't get time to whip out a book and start analyzing people's faces during a conversation, so the book is there for you to look at in your spare time. You could also try turning the sound down completely on the television to see if you can understand the storyline just by watching the actors' gestures and expressions. The box on the page opposite will help you to read the most common gestures people make, even if you can't always use the gestures properly yourself.

Sending the right signals

Using body language properly is more difficult than understanding it. I can't walk and talk properly at the same time – if I do, I lose the ability to walk in a straight line and start bashing the person I'm talking to with my elbows. This must make me seem a little aggressive and rude, so I have to pay attention to what my limbs are doing. Slouching apparently means that you are bored, so if you have postural difficulties take care to straighten up when someone is talking to you.

You should also make noises like, 'Hmm,' and nod your head to show that you're interested in a conversation. Do this even if you are being bored out of your mind, and try not to let your attention wander. Quite often my brain has a power surge of thoughts and I walk off right when someone is speaking to me, to do whatever it is I've just thought of. I don't mean to be bad mannered. The other person's words trickle out of my ears and I forget where I am.

It's important that you end conversations in a friendly way. If your brain really is nagging you to get away, or if either you or the other person has had enough, finish with a smile and something like, 'I've enjoyed this' or, 'See you soon'. Now you are allowed to clear off!

Gesture	Translation
Shaking a finger	'I'm warning you' or 'You've done something I don't approve of'. (This signal can be used jokingly.)
Drawing a finger across the throat	'Stop, or you'll be in trouble.' (Also used humorously.)
Clenched fist	'I'm angry.' (In winter, this could simply mean that the person's hands are cold.)
Arms crossed over chest	'I'd rather not be having this conversation' or 'I'm feeling unsure' or 'I'm cold'.
Palms open	'I'm receptive and welcoming.'
Palms steepled in a prayer position and held in lap	'I'm confident.'
Feet pointing towards you	'I'm listening and I'm interested.'
One foot pointing away from you	'I'd rather be going.'
Feet apart and hands on hips	'I'm angry.'
Comfortably slouching in a chair or against a wall	'I'm relaxing' or sometimes 'I'm bored'.
Chin up, staring, hands on hips	'I'm feeling stubborn and I will do whatever I like.'

Finding friends

My occupational therapist gave lots of helpful tips on how to get organized...then, quite off the subject and quite apart from her expertise, I asked her about my main problem – socializing. I wanted to know what I was doing wrong, and to my great surprise she told me I was doing nothing wrong! Unnoticed by me I had matured a lot and was now a polite, sensible, if a little quiet young lady. The occupational therapist told me that it wasn't my fault and I would find many friends as soon as they'd matured. From then on forward, things got better.

Hannah, 16

Like me, all my friends have been made to another recipe. We add our own zest to the world and we can accept and understand (OK, maybe we don't go that far!) each other's differences. If you feel better around people who have your sort of difficulties, you could log onto the Internet and pay a visit to the Dyspraxic Teens' website. A bunch of us recently decided to set up our own support group on the web. It's nice to know that there is an understanding ear to turn to whenever things get too much, and the group has been a lifeline for me.

But we can't stay locked up in our wonderful dyspraxic world forever. Happily, people become much more tolerant and open-minded as they grow older and your differences may not be such an obstacle once you reach your late teens. You could also try joining some clubs to help you to make friends with other people who have similar interests. The more specialized an activity is, the more likely you are to meet people who are like you – after all, it takes an insane breed of person (possibly with a collective death wish) to want to go crawling around narrow tunnels underground! For example, on my compound in Saudi there is a group of fast friends who are united by their desire to go scuba diving and feed sharks with bloodied chickens.

CHAPTER 6

The Case of the Cooked Tomato

The lunatic, the lover, and the poet are in imagination all compact.

William Shakespeare, A Midsummer Night's Dream

Love and lunacy

We now make the rather large leap from chickens to relationships. I will admit here and now that I have just as much expertise on this subject as I do on the chickens, but with the patient help of a select group of non-dyspraxic people, I think I've made a fairly decent job of this.

How to tell when you like someone

This seems like a pretty pointless subheading. I wouldn't bother writing it if I hadn't liked someone for months without realizing it, but I assume there must be a handful of other mad people around. When you're around someone you like, your face is liable to flame up like a frying tomato (a big evolutionary mistake – doing an impersonation of a traffic light on 'stop' may have been thought attractive in caveman days, but in the twenty-first century it's embarrassing) and you may feel as if there is an eggbeater churning up your insides. You will like thinking about the person. You will find your legs walking to areas where you know they hang out. Your eyes covertly scan a classroom for the divine presence before you sit down. And however much you inwardly scream at yourself to call a halt, you can't stop.

Many adolescents with dyspraxia seem to be immune to their own hormones. Until I turned sixteen I had no idea what it felt like to be attracted to someone. I was vaguely aware that there were items called boys wandering about somewhere on the other side of whatever book I happened to be reading, but they were of no interest to me. Then one day, wham! My immunity failed, my knees dissolved into blancmange, my face blazed like a stewed plum and I felt as if someone had turned my head upside-down and given my thoughts a good shaking. I had so many other things to think about (such as passing my exams and remembering to give in my homework and getting up the language block's staircase without breaking my neck) that further complications were definitely *not* on the programme.

Because of our social differences, most dyspraxic teen-agers aren't prepared to cope with this sudden onslaught of foreign thoughts and feelings. How do you approach someone whom you like? The conversation must surely change – are there any special rules for that? What's this person trying to say? And finally, supposing you do end up with a person whom you like, what about stuff like kissing?

I don't know whether this is because I grew up in an Islamic country or because I am a private person, but the very idea of having someone so physically close to me makes me feel nauseated. People with dyspraxia often have sensory problems that make physical contact difficult to tolerate and many of us hate being crowded. The tips here are just guiding signposts, to stop us from getting too lost if we do find ourselves in this confusing maze. Like me, you may want to save them for later.

Tips to help

- Calm down! If you don't think your actions through carefully you're going to do something rash, like walking up to a friend when she's talking to your victim and saying, 'Hands off, he's reserved property'. Er, not that I did that, of course.

- Do your research. If you don't already know, find out what the person's interests are. If you love chess and the victim is in the Chess Club, join it...

- ...but if you really hate chess, don't. Always be yourself.

- Does your potential victim struggle with a subject that you are conveniently good at? If they do, you could offer to help them.

- If you have friends who won't blab to everyone, send them off to reconnoitre. I have done this. (Thanks, Emma!) The only problem is that they will probably want to set you up without delay – something I hadn't bargained for – so be prepared to cope with an army of pushy matchmakers.

- Be careful about flirting. I still don't have a very good idea of what this is. I have observed other girls when they do what they call 'flirting' and there is a lot of laughing hysterically and tossing your ponytail about involved. I don't see how this is attractive.

- Oh, wait, we have a fresh bulletin from the non-dyspraxic advice panel. It assures me that eye contact (ugh) is crucial. Try looking someone in the eyes, then glancing nervously away, then looking back.

- Always be polite. Non-dyspraxic boys especially appear to think that a great way to attract someone is to scream out remarks about their body. This isn't flattering or funny. It will embarrass people.

- If they are clearly terrified, it could be that they like you and are shy about it, or that they can't stand this treatment any more. You can either:

  1. wait for them to make the next move. This is a coward's escape route but it is distinctly safer than to...

  2. corner them, take a deep breath, declare how you feel, and ask if they feel the same way. If yes, the conversation should go from there. (Well, I can't continue with this advice guide right up until your wedding day!) If no, at least the nail-biting wait will be done with, and you won't be wasting your time any more.

DCD can trip you up (literally) when you find yourself in this embarrassing situation. I was with my victim in the library, 'sitting' on a swivel chair. I nearly fell into his lap twice and I think I managed to terrify him witless for a week. The non-dyspraxic advice panel assures me that this was the best thing I could have done, but I wouldn't personally recommend it!

If you do decide to try out the above tips, the other person might not react in the way you envisaged. Even if your potential victim does return your feelings, they are unlikely to just blurt it out – especially if they are male. Lads, dyspraxic or otherwise, seem to be completely unable to open their mouths and coherently articulate what is going on in their minds when they fancy someone. Any boys who are reading this, please make a special effort not to speak in gasps and monosyllables when you're talking to a girl you like. She won't attack you, but she might be tempted to if you aren't a bit more vocal. As for non-dyspraxic girls, they seem to like flicking their hair about and throwing darting glances at the object of desire to get their message across. Given that most of us don't notice people's faces and wouldn't understand what their eyebrows were saying even if we did, it would be better if you could somehow explain to your potential victim that you like things clear and explicit.

The inability to understand body language can be very useful in this situation. When you are near someone you fancy, your brain might decide to take a holiday to Baffin Island and leave you blinking stupidly like a rabbit caught in the headlights. If by any chance you do manage to pick up on the other person's non-verbal signals, you can pretend not to understand what's going on and force them to make the first move. This isn't being sly and brutal. This is self-preservation at all costs!

The dating game

- Be as confident as you can. All teenagers are nervous and embarrassed when they like someone.

- When you meet the person, try and get a casual compliment in. I say 'casual', because if you start spouting Shakespeare's 'Shall I compare thee to a summer's day?' their reaction will probably be to run to Timbuktu.

- If you are the brave person who actually did the asking out, you should offer to pay (providing you aren't visiting a very expensive place). If the other person wants to pay for him or herself, then buy them a snack.

- Ask the person where they want to go and what they would like to do, to show them that they are important to you.

- Conversational rules still apply. Listen attentively when the person is speaking. If you get restless easily, do your best not to fidget.

- If you have a favourite topic that obsesses you, try not to talk about it all the time. Over the years I have sadly resigned myself to the fact that most people don't want to discuss character development in *David Copperfield*.

- Kissing is a whole new area and a very foreign one. It is, unfortunately, one of those things that requires some co-ordination, understanding of body language and social judgement. The advice panel suggests that you be gentle and don't kiss the person's lips immediately – see if they're OK with you kissing their cheek first. If they are…then the rest is personal and can't really be covered by a bullet-pointed list on dyspraxic dating.

- If you are uncomfortable when being touched or kissed, don't put up with it. Move away. You don't have to do anything you don't like. Trust your gut instinct if you are unsure.

- The same rule goes if the other person is the one who is uncomfortable with your advances. If they don't like being touched (check the body language translator chart in the previous chapter for what they might be trying to say) then do respect their feelings.

- Personal things are best kept quiet! If you have a best friend whom you have known long enough to trust it would probably be OK to discuss your date with them, but definitely no one else.

A lot of teenagers act like they are planning a military campaign when they fancy someone. Night after night I see hordes of boarding house girls brewing up gallons of hot chocolate and settling down at a table to avidly discuss pulling strategies. When I was doing research for this chapter, I listened to several of these battle plans and came away feeling very puzzled. When parties or discos roll round, each girl even works out a back-up strategy: 'If I can't get with Paul, I'll try Joe…' I can't know for certain, but I have a hunch that most boys also make up mental lists of possible choices. This makes it sound as if people are like second-hand clothes that can be swapped and shared. I don't understand how anyone could fancy a person they barely know. If you want a relationship to last, it is good to be on friendly terms with the other person before you start going out. If you're already friends with them, you are free to act as you normally would and the whole thing isn't quite so complicated and confusing. I have a strong suspicion that people make all this much more complex than it really needs to be, just out of a taste for drama.

It may be hard to think along these logical lines when you're in the presence of someone you like. I'm not a robot, much as I would sometimes like to be one (if I could somehow control my blushing it would be a big plus) and my body seems to develop a mind of its own in certain circumstances. Isn't it strange when you suddenly find yourself swamped with a burning desire to hug someone, and yet you know that if you gave in to the urge, your nerve receptors would be squealing, 'Skin – ugh!'?

Not all DCD people have this problem. In fact, some of us are much too tactile. Everything seems to be extreme with us. I can't emphasize enough how important it is to be careful when touching or hugging someone. Boys with dyspraxia should be really cautious here. If you have problems grading your movements and can't judge your own strength, you'll end up scaring whoever it is that you are hugging. You might not want to talk about dyspraxia on a date (it's not the best chat-up line in the world) but you will probably both feel more comfortable if she knows that you are clumsy.

You cannot serve two gods...

Last week I was talking about the 2004 shortlist for the Carnegie Medalwith the school librarian, and we came across a novel called *A Gathering Light*[*]. One reviewer had written, 'If George Clooney had come into the room while I was reading this I would have told him to go away and come back when I had finished'. Mrs C crowed with delight and declared, 'This must be a winner. Not many books make you feel like that!'

I favoured her with one of my hard over-the-glasses stares. 'Are you honestly saying that you would put a male – *any* male – before your divine calling as librarian?'

'Weellll...yes. Don't look at me like that! You'll feel differently in a few years!'

---

*   This book, by Jennifer Donnelly, did win the Carnegie Medal.

Ironically, the main character in *A Gathering Light* believes that it is impossible to have both love and books. Many teenagers with dyspraxia have one or two things that fascinate them, such as computers or art or drama – I've even met one girl who is obsessed with spoons – and when a fascination fills your head there is very little room for anything else. There is a person who, at the time of writing, occupies the few brain cells that aren't reserved for books, but liking someone does not necessarily mean that you want to go out with them. Yet maybe Mrs C is right. Maybe I will one day catch up with other girls my age and talk about nothing but rugby players' legs. But for the moment I fail to see the attraction in a tangle of hairy limbs that are normally coated in mud and clods of grassy earth. The Sahara will freeze over and become a municipal skating-rink before I put anything like that before my books.

CHAPTER 7

Bullying

Life is mostly froth and bubble,
Two things stand in stone,
Kindness in another's trouble,
Courage in your own.
  Adam Lindsay Gordon, Ye Wearie Way Farer

Warning signs to watch for

Bullying is a well-worn patch in the dyspraxic tapestry. People who have different coloured skin, foreigners, those who practise another religion, people who wear glasses, people with beaky noses, people with freckled faces – you're all different from me, so I will make sure that I hurt and terrify you as much as I can.

This is a bully's logic. Those of us with learning differences often stick out like a fistful of sore thumbs so we're immediately at risk from people who think in this senseless way. But if you look closely you will notice something else about the bullying logic: it could be the person with DCD who is the bully.

At one of my schools in Saudi Arabia there was a boy named Liam. No one liked him much. That wasn't surprising, as he was one of the

105

biggest bullies in the school. He used to slash at younger children with a badminton racket and threaten others with an arsenal of foul language. He was hopeless at PE, his handwriting looked like an inky centipede had staggered across the page, and when his work was put on the wall you could see where he had reversed letters. I wasn't fond of Liam either but I felt a strange kind of solidarity with him that I struggled to understand. This made me like him even less. Who likes to think that they've got things in common with the class bully?

Strangely, he left me alone. He never bothered my friend Sara either, who missed out chunks of text when she read aloud and whose work crawled with spelling mistakes. Now I know that Liam could easily have had dyslexia and DCD and I feel very ashamed. I don't know where he is now but I hope he got the help he needed.

The symptoms

At home:

- I'm having trouble sleeping and sometimes get nightmares.
- I don't have the energy to do anything anymore.
- I swing from wanting to cry to feeling really irritable and argumentative.
- My appetite changes – I either want to stuff myself with food, or not eat at all.
- I need to take extra money because the bullies have threatened to hurt me if I don't give them cash.
- I don't enjoy my favourite activities any more.
- I feel as if my parents don't understand. I sometimes want to be close to them and other times I just want to be alone.
- My family notices that I don't bring any friends home or go to parties.
- I have to take the long way to school to avoid Them. It's hard to think up a good explanation for why I have to do this.

At school:

- My school stuff is often taken and spoilt.

- Teachers ask me about cuts and bruises and I feel worried, because I can't say how I got them.

- Some kids order me about and others laugh at me.

- I have to take a long time when I pack up at the end of a lesson, so I can leave when the teacher does.

- My grades are going down and I'm scared to speak up in class.

- People titter and whisper when I do ask a question or make a point.

- I am always the last one chosen for the team.

- I'm taunted for being poor at team sports and other lessons.

- I get pushed and shoved at in queues or in the corridors.

- Doors are slammed in my face.

- People ignore me when I'm speaking or shout out insults.

The bully and the bullied

> My sensitivity and misinterpretation of what others said to me made me seem 'weird'. I'd constantly say and do the wrong things, which made me seem like a horrible person. My bad reputation worsened as I got into fights at my new primary school. One day I was slowly getting changed in the changing rooms, feeling sorry for myself again. I was the last person in the room apart from one girl who, for no particular reason, started calling me. I snapped. Over six years later people still label me as a bully, as the poor girl whom I fought had suffered injuries to the skull. When she came to my secondary school she got not only her year, but sixth formers, parts of the boys' division, and even the junior division to hate and despise me. I have been in many fights like this. And so my reputation worsened and worsened.

My self-esteem hit rock bottom at my new secondary school, when the only friend I had broke up with me, saying she was only friends with me because she 'felt sorry' for me. But it was pity that won me my first true friend, Pippa. I was sitting alone eating my school dinner and she was on a table surrounded by friends. Out of pity she invited me to her table and we got on like a house on fire. But she was in the year above me so we didn't get to see much of each other, the way my school regimented everything. Even other pupils tried to separate us. I burn with the injustice of it when my whole form objected to Pippa visiting me in form time. They said she disrupted the rest of the form, which was entirely hypocritical since many of their friends who entered the room shouted and screamed like howler monkeys! Then, because I was weird, and because I had a friend, and because it was an all-girls' school, the rumour went around that I was a lesbian. It lasted for so long that I myself wondered whether it was true, until it came to the ridiculous point where I was afraid to hug my own mother.

Hannah, 16

The bit I don't want to write

If someone had presented me with the tips below when I was at my last school I would have used them to line my cat's litter tray. When there is a group of people who seem to enjoy nothing more than making your life hell it's difficult to keep your cool. When I turned twelve, we moved from the city of Jeddah to a small town in the Hijaz Mountains of Arabia. I was thrilled at the idea of going to a new school where no one would know about my difficulties, and I resolved to work frantically to push my grades up. I was going to make friends. This time I really was going to try hard.

It didn't take long for that idea to shrivel up. The bullying at my new school was worse than it had ever been. I was subjected to a barrage of taunts and name-calling, my beloved books were stolen and ripped apart, I was pushed down the stairs and – worst of all, as I'm afraid of spiders – someone put a very realistic photo in my desk. I had to run to the toilet to throw up. The old adage 'sticks and stones will break my bones, but words will never hurt me' is totally stupid. Words, unlike bruises, never fade away. They are seared into your memory forever.

Each day I walked into what felt like the jaws of hell. Nausea was clotting in my throat and my hands were sticky with sweat before the bus got halfway to school. It's a horrible feeling, isn't it? To reach my locker, I had to pass through a gang of sniggering girls in the year above who always huddled in the doorway before school. I didn't know their names. They would adopt nasally posh accents as I walked by, tug at my schoolbag, and pull out strands of my hair. I ignored them. As the door swung shut behind me they burst into loud laughter. It got so bad that I couldn't bear to hear anyone laughing, convinced that they had to be laughing at me. Whenever someone called me, my name usually had an obscenity attached to it. Some of the milder nouns that were substituted for 'Vicky' were 'reject', 'spaz', and 'retard'. The words rang in my ears at night when I tried to sleep. I could never escape them. In the end, I started to believe they were true.

I get so angry when I hear people – mostly adults – talking about how it is good for a child to be bullied so that he or she can learn to deal with conflict in the 'real world'. I wonder if these philosophers were ever bullied themselves? Somehow I think not, or else they would surely know that cutting words and sly pinches are very real. I can now do a brilliant break-fall and I know how to escape from someone who is gripping me by the neck or hair, but I don't see how these skills are going to brighten up my CV in later life! Another idea that sends hot currents of anger fizzing through my blood is the idea that children who are bullied are somehow to blame, as they are too sensitive and they ask for it. I thought my ears were malfunctioning when I first heard this one. No one asks for free accommodation in purgatory. Bullying is never, ever your fault.

I wish I had known that then. No one else in my class is treated like this, I realized, so I must be a bad person who deserves punishment. I punctured my skin with my nails, forced myself to go without food, and made myself wake up at strange hours to punish myself. In a strange way the sight of blood beading on the welts in my flesh made me feel much better (though I wouldn't recommend this as a coping strategy). I sometimes wet my bed and felt ill in the night. It's easy to say, 'Tell your parents,' but no thirteen-year-old likes to admit that she's in this kind of mess. Stupid as it may sound, I had my pride.

I also strongly believe that what goes around comes around. Now I can only feel sorry that the people who put us in these positions will one day have a lot to answer for.

In spite of this comforting belief I wish I had talked about it more. Bringing it all out into the open would have been nothing compared to everything else that went on. Please tell someone you can trust. Now that it is all behind me, I wish so much that I had ended it sooner. No one can spend her life with her nails pressed into her skin. Please go on. You can do it.

Advice for the victim

- Firstly and most importantly, you must understand that *this is not your fault*. Being different is no justification for bullying. Never let anyone convince you otherwise.

- Never try to ignore the problem in the hope of it going away. It won't disappear overnight.

- Tell a trusted adult (or several) at once. Bullies may promise dire things if you grass them up, but how much power does a gang of teenagers have in real life? To look at it objectively – bog all. Bullies are cowards. If you bring in someone who has more power than they do (and that shouldn't be hard) they will scatter like the woolly-headed sheep that they are.

- Whenever you need moral support, phone Childline or come and find us on the Dyspraxic Teens' website. Let your feelings go.

- Keep a diary of all the incidents as they happen. This will help your teachers if they want to know about each event. It will also allow you to vent frustration and help you to think clearly.

- At breaks and lunchtimes try and find a safe harbour. The library is a good place to head. Don't hang around the toilets or in hidden away, isolated places. Ironically, the areas that you think are safe hideouts are actually the places that bullies are most likely to check.

- Keep close to a friend if you have one. If not, are there any other people in your class who are also targeted? See if you can stick with them at breaks and lunches. Safety lies in numbers.

- If you are being bullied physically, do not hit back. If they can make you give up your self-possession then they are winning this fight. They want to provoke you because it's their idea of fun. Don't let them succeed.

- There's one exception to this rule. If you are in an isolated place where no one can hear you and it is a choice between you getting hurt or them, then make sure it is them. I once had to resort to hitting someone in the face just to escape, and while I am not proud of this escapade it was the only thing I could have done. Don't fight for the heck of it. Get away as soon as you can.

- If you are being verbally abused, look bored. Nod and say, 'Uh-huh, whatever you say' whenever they come out with a fresh insult. This technique is normally too much for their tiny minds to fathom. 'Huh? He's not getting upset or angry? What's going on?'

- If the bullies attack your 'stupidity' ('Can't you even write your name yet, thicko?') come back with something like, 'No, but at least I know what it is!'

- Crowds of bullies are harder to deal with, especially if they're all making noise at once. Try to calm down. Take a deep breath and leave the room. If they are hemming you in, remain self-possessed. Speak politely and try not to show fear. (And yes, I do know how hard that is!) You can think much more clearly if you are calm.

- If you shuffle about with your shoulders hunched and your eyes fixed on the toes of your shoes, you are sending out the message, 'Hey, I'm an easy target! Line up to bully!' Body language may be difficult for you to work out, but try to take big confident strides and to hold your head up high.

- The bully may be as afraid as you are. Some bullies only do what they do simply because they have problems of their own. If you know that your particular tormentor is having a hard time, the best way to floor them is to show some genuine sympathy. One of my old primary school bullies ended up as a semi-friend once I realized that he was human.

Bullies in high places

> Year 7 [age 11–12] was when it got a whole lot worse. I was bullied very badly and my organizational problems were worsened by secondary school. The most the school and my parents could do was tell me I had low self-esteem because of the dyspraxia. The school told me it was my fault that I was bullied, because I was too passive or something. I don't know how they managed to blame it on me. My teachers weren't helpful either.
>
> *Lucinda, 15*

Sadly, scarily, not all teachers are supportive of pupils who are being bullied. Some may actively participate in the abuse.

- Always be polite to the teacher in question. If they insult you but you are quietly polite in response then they will look like a twit in front of the rest of the class, and they hate this. I know it works.

- Write down a list of things that the teacher has done that you feel constitute bullying. Date each event. Your parents can then show this to the head teacher.

- If the bully is your form tutor then your parents can request that you be moved to another form.

- If the problem persists then your parents or carer can approach the school governors. They have a duty to look into problems like this.

- Are there any pupils in your class who would be prepared to anonymously report what the teacher has done? It is best for the head teacher or the deputy to approach individual members of the class with this request, emphasizing that the information will be treated in strict confidence.

The last resort

Swapping schools or choosing home education are always possibilities. Several DCD children, including me, have had to do one or the other. This may feel like running away, but when you've done everything you possibly can and nothing's working, you need to get out.

An important thing to remember here is that 'bullies' are not always what they seem. Some dyspraxic kids may not be too good at working out when someone is teasing or just being friendly. If you don't like something that is happening, explain nicely to the person that you'd rather they didn't do it. If they really are being friendly then they'll understand. I have been badly mistaken over people's intentions in the past, accusing them of insulting me when all they were trying to do was make friends. But generally, if you feel upset about something that has happened, then it *is* bullying. Trust your gut. (That's one saying I definitely don't get – what have a person's intestines got to do with cognitive processes?) A handful of teachers try to use the 'They-were-just-messing-about' spiel as an excuse to do nothing. If you really do feel hurt then this is not an answer.

You might even need to get professional help if you've been badly hurt by this. There's only so much that a list of anti-bullying tips and a friendly voice can do. Some people think that DCD is the only problem we have, which is completely untrue. Dyspraxia itself is a talent; bullying is one unfair price that we pay. If things ever get so bad that you think of taking your own life – and this has happened in the past – then pause for thought. Talk to a parent or speak to a friend. I say this for two reasons. No bully is powerful enough to drive you to this extreme, even though his or her actions may have blinded your reasoning skills and convinced you otherwise. Bullying doesn't last forever. Secondly, you are an amazing person and the world would be much poorer if it didn't have you in it.

Advice for the bully

- The first step is the hardest. If you are hurting someone then you are in the wrong and you need to apologise. Generously. A muttered 'Sorry' isn't enough. If you feel unable to apologise to your victim's face, put it in a letter.

- Are you part of a gang and afraid they'll turn on you if you do what you know to be right? The right choice isn't an easy one to make. Take a deep breath and go for it.

- Get some support behind you before you do this. Good teachers understand that it is just as upsetting to bully as to be bullied, and they will help you.

- You may not be actively participating in bullying, but standing by and watching it go on is bad enough.

- Bullying does not equal power. It will not make you popular.

- Don't be afraid. You are not a horrible person – and your victim isn't the freak that you have made him feel like. It's time you realized both things.

Having a learning difficulty and always being the odd one out is enough to make anyone feel insecure. But 'understandable' and 'acceptable' are two completely different things and being unhappy yourself doesn't give you the right to inflict utter despair on someone else. A lot of bullies who have special needs go by the principle 'I'll get them before they can get me'. I feel desperately sorry for kids like this as they have no sense of trust.

   If you are constantly urging yourself to act more 'normal' then you are chasing after a pipe dream. When no two people are alike, how can a normal state even exist? People who are comfortable with themselves and with others are those who understand and appreciate the variety in the world. We aren't identical factory-made dolls. There is diversity wherever you turn your head, and you mustn't let your difference scare you into hurting someone else.

Words of wisdom for people in power

Parents:

- Don't shout at your child for keeping the bullying a secret. He's clearly getting enough of this at school. Remember that some adolescents with dyspraxia are unable to understand the difference between bullying and teasing, so they might not even think of mentioning what's going on to you, assuming that it's normal.

- Watch closely for the bullying symptoms, remembering that they may not all be present. People react to stress in different ways.

- Ask your child to talk about his or her feelings. They may feel more comfortable speaking to a sibling, but never mind this so long as they have a chance to vent their feelings, and you have an opportunity to work out how to handle the situation.

- Never, ever tell the child to 'go with the flow' or suggest that he or she try to act a bit more like everyone else. We shouldn't have to conform to someone else's idea of normal just to feel safe. If a one-legged child got bullied because of his handicap, nobody would expect him to sprout another limb in order to fit in!

- Call a parent–teacher meeting and ask to hear the school's bullying policies.

- Consider meeting with the bully's parents to discuss the matter. You should arrange this through the school. Don't be aggressive. The bully's parents might be ignorant of their child's behaviour – bullies don't taunt people right outside their parents' front window.

- Ask any older siblings who also attend the school to act as their brother or sister's watchdogs.

- Severe cases of bullying warrant the interference of the police. Don't rule this out as an option. There have been suicides as a result of bullying before now.

- If you send your child to school when he's facing serious bullying, then you're sending him into the fire. Keep him away until things are sorted. This isn't cowardice. My parents had to do this for me at one point, and although I ended up missing more than a few days (it took six months to get me into Colditz) I didn't turn into a juvenile delinquent. If your kid is being badly bullied he is probably too distraught to learn much anyway. You can't concentrate on your work when you know you have hell to pay at lunch.

Teachers:

- Please understand that bullying is a big problem for 'different' kids. We can't help the way we think and we can't always follow other people's conversations, so in many cases of bullying a dyspraxic kid genuinely won't know how to behave. If you can understand this then the problem is already half-solved.

- Crack down quickly and let the student body – and the staff – know that bullying of any description won't be tolerated.

- Assure your class that anyone is always welcome to come to you and talk about bullying problems.

- Identify 'at risk' pupils and keep a discreet eye out for them at break times and lunches. If you want to catch a bully red-handed, remember that you won't be able to do it from the staff room window.

- Set up a support system in school. Maybe older teenagers would be willing to act as mentors to the lower school, as kids might feel better about talking to someone close to them in age.

- Let the class know that bullying doesn't just affect the victim, but the class as a whole. Drama lessons are a good place to get this message across. You could use role-plays and centre the day's group work round the bullying theme.

- Be aware that in most schools Personal, Social, Health Education (PSHE) lessons are a joke. If you want to deliver your anti-bullying message in one of these classes, make sure that you come up with something better than circle time. A teenager who is being bullied will not volunteer to talk about his problems if the antagonist is staring at him from across the circle. Would you?

- Gather newspaper cuttings about deaths and suicides that have occurred as a result of bullying and discuss them. Maybe not even the bullies realize that their actions could trigger something so serious.

- Be aware that members of your own staff are not infallible and some of them could be guilty of contributing to a particular child's misery. Teachers may need more training in order to fully understand that DCD kids aren't just lazy or antisocial. An out-of-school professional could come in to deliver a talk on a Teacher Training Day – the British Dyslexia Association can supply lecturers.

- Remember that the bully will also need help sorting out his or her problems.

Ideally you should stop bullying before it even begins. Prevention is better than cure. Often teachers encourage pupils to bully classmates with DCD without realizing what they're doing. Pinning a dyspraxic pupil's work to the wall when he can't control his pen properly is like pinning up his death warrant. Criticizing him for handing in said work late, forgetting his belongings, and not paying attention in class is teaching his peers to think of him as stupid. Don't highlight his differences in front of the class in this way.

A blank page to write on

Bullying maliciously worms its way into every area of your life. Sometimes it feels like it will be with you forever, but I can promise you that it will end some day. Before you get angry and start thinking, 'Huh, she doesn't know anything about me,' I'm going to contradict you and say yes, I do! At least, I may not know you personally but I know what your situation feels like. Even though they may act like they're invincible, every bully gets caught out. I would have given anything to know this at my last school. My parents kept telling it to me but I wouldn't listen. I wanted it to end *now*, not 'one day'. 'One day' isn't good enough when your every waking moment is taken up by worry over what's going to happen next – and besides, I don't have much concept of time. But by using the tips above and getting as much help as possible, you can bring that day closer. You are not alone.

Matthew's story

By March 2001, school had become unbearable. I was regularly punched and kicked by the bullies and had to tolerate constant verbal abuse and could not concentrate on my work. At home I was having nightmares, I wasn't eating properly, felt depressed and at times felt like killing myself. I just shut myself away in my room and listened to my Robbie Williams CDs, hoping someone would take the pain away. Something had to be done and as the school were unwilling to accept that I needed help, my parents were left to make a difficult decision. After much discussion and research it was decided I would come out of school and on 6 April 2001 I officially left school and began home education.

My sister still goes to the school where I suffered at the hands of the bullies, and I sometimes feel guilty, because she is hassled by the same children. They tell her that they miss kicking my head in. I still see them sometimes when I take my dog for a walk. They swear at me, threaten me, and refer to incidents that happened at school. They seem proud of what they did, which means the school not only let me down but let them down too, which makes me sad.

Today I am different from the sad, demoralized, and scared person I was when I left school for the last time. I feel stronger and have a better sense of my purpose in life. The next few years are like a blank page for me to write and I am looking forward to all the opportunities that may come to me.

Matthew, 14

CHAPTER 8

Coping with Growing Up

Adolescence is when children start bringing up their parents.

Anonymous

Most teenagers appear to be obsessed with growing up. When I first arrived in Colditz it seemed that everywhere I went people were commenting on the size of others' body parts and avidly discussing personal (very personal) topics. Not for nothing is our common room known as 'the antisocial room'. If parents knew what goes on at the average British school they would probably lock us up until we hit eighteen, which is why I had better move swiftly on…

Dyspraxia does seem to get worse in the teenage years and there are many reasons for this. First off, we get no dispensation on the hormonal front. Hormones and special needs are not a great combination, as I (not to mention my family) know very well. I spent years trying to talk myself into liking skating and handstands because all the other children did these things, and just as I thought I'd managed to strike a compromise between fitting in and doing my own thing, the rules of the game changed. The boys started to gel their hair and the girls came to school wearing makeup. Hold on, when did this happen?! My attention was soon diverted by the unpredictable growth of my limbs, which seemed to lengthen by four feet in the space of a week. My hands were too far away to be of any earthly use and I was forever breaking things. Furniture. Crockery. My arm. The teeth of the sixth-form games captain. (I didn't punch her, I just lost control of my hockey stick.)

Having a disability opens up a set of new physical and emotional needs that other adolescents don't even have to think about. Negotiating these obstacles is tough and it is also a solitary journey. Most of us do not want herds of advisors stampeding through this sensitive area, reminiscing about their own adolescence, least of all their teenage body odour problems. (*Cough,* certain school nurses need to take note. Disciple Jill this means you, *cough-cough.*)

Dressing hang-ups

> When jeans came into fashion I was left out of it. I NEVER wore jeans or any other fabric that didn't feel right against my skin, this made shopping for me very difficult and when the school held 'jeans for genes' days or even just non-uniform days absolutely EVERYONE wore jeans, except me. As I've grown older I have managed to overcome this obstacle too – when I was fourteen I wore my first pair of jeans since I was a toddler. Now I follow most fashions and am starting to fit in.
>
> *Hannah, 16*

- Look for clothes that are easy to put on.

- Make sure that you can cope with the texture of the material.

- Attach a zip-puller or a thin bit of fabric to your zip to make it easier to fasten.

- Lay out your clothes for the next day in the correct order to save morning stress.

- Sit down to put on pullovers and sweatshirts to stop you getting disorientated and falling over.

- Tie shoelaces using the bunny method. Fold each lace back on itself to form a loop that looks like a rabbit's ear, then tie the two together.

- There are Bungee laces available from some shops that need one twist to tie them. They come in lots of colours. Thin black elastic also looks sufficiently like laces to be worn for school – get someone to tie the shoes for you, and from then on just slip them on and off.

- You can cheat with school ties. There are 'fake' ties available that are attached to a piece of elastic. Pull the string over your head, tuck it under your collar, and *voila*. (These are good, as unlike normal ties they don't make you feel as if you have a noose around your neck.) Or you could ask someone to fasten your tie for you, and then get them to cut it in half at the back. Sew a Velcro patch to each end. The tie stays knotted and you use the Velcro to put it on.

- Remember that buttonholes at the top of shirts and most collared blouses are stitched horizontally instead of vertically. This convinces me that the sole purpose of clothing manufacturers is to confuse us!

- If you have trouble with telling the time, a digital watch is easier to read than a conventional one. There are bracelet watches and watches with elasticized straps that are easy to slip on and off.

- If you want to wear jewellery or other accessories, pick out items that have large clasps or are elasticized, unless you can get someone to fasten them for you.

- Attach your locker or house-key to your belt with a curly cord. Make sure you have a spare set of keys in your schoolbag.

Dress codes and colour co-ordination

Some of us have problems picking up on acceptable dress codes and end up wandering through public places looking like a can of paint crossed with a zebra. In my little corner of England the entire population seems to have this problem so one solitary DCD teenager doesn't stick out too much! But if you have trouble choosing the 'right' clothes you may attract more teasing at a time when your social skills aren't that good to begin with. At the beginning of secondary school in Jeddah I had more important things to think about than what I wore and I used to stroll about in my auntie's old floral skirts. Not something I'd recommend that you do!

- Ask someone to tell you whether colours match or not.

- It's easier to match clothes and colours when they're off your person.

- Think of the places where you are planning to wear certain outfits. Is a Manchester City football shirt appropriate gear for a visit to the Manchester United stadium, and is that halter-top really OK for a prayer service?

- If you have your own distinctive style and you know it's not offensive, wear it with pride. I sometimes get weird looks when I dress in a sari or a *salwar-kameez* in the boarding house, but most people have better things to do than scrutinize my fashion sense. And if they don't, it's not my wardrobe that is at fault, but their boring lives. Don't be afraid to be original.

Health and hygiene

Check that your bathroom is dyspraxic-friendly. Showers are dangerous places and it's too easy to fall over and hurt yourself. I once ended up with a spectacular turtle-shaped bruise on my backside and it is not an experience you want to share, so:

- Have a handrail beside the toilet.

- Have a stool or a bath-board in the tub, so you can sit if your balance is poor.

- Use shower gels instead of soap – bottles are easier to grip.

- Look out for bottles and containers that are easy to open and squeeze.

- Wash your hair at least three times a week, more if it needs it, and take a shower daily. For some reason adolescents with DCD seem to sweat more. (Don't we have all the luck!)

- Keep a timer in the bathroom so you don't lose track of how long you've been in the shower.

- Roll-on deodorants don't need as much co-ordination as spray-on ones. You don't want to end up deodorizing your eyes.

- Line up all your toiletries in the order that you will use them.

- Sometimes you might lose track of what you're doing in the shower and forget whether you've washed your hair or not, so stick to a set routine and transfer your soaps and bottles to a different part of the tub when you've finished with them. Have a laminated list of procedures or waterproof scuba-diving slate (Wash face, soap body, wash hair...) that you can refer to as you go.

- Some of us can't cope with showering – the water itches your skin and the noise is irritating. Taking a bath is less painful.

- Nails should be cut cleanly straight across and scrubbed with a flannel to remove dirt. Could a parent help you to cut your toenails, if you are worried about amputating your foot? If not, a rough emery board is a good substitute for nail-cutting. It has to be done more often than trimming but it comes without the risk of finishing up three-toed.

Using the toilet

Umm, I won't go into detail on this topic, but going to the toilet may still be a problem for you because of the balance, body awareness, and muscle control that it takes. A lot of my teachers still don't understand that when I ask to be excused, I mean I want to go *now*, and no, I can't wait until break! My parents are very familiar with this problem, as when we're driving through the desert in Saudi I nearly always end up having to crouch behind the car while my mum keeps watch for passing goatherds and low-flying aircraft. If there are any teachers reading this, please make sure that pupils with DCD know exactly where the toilets are. It is so easy to get lost when every corridor looks alike and you can't picture building plans mentally. Difficulties with orientation usually result in a panicked stagger round school in cross-legged agony, something that can cause a nasty accident!

These accidents are not something that the average teenager will talk about. What fourteen-year-old is going to put soiled underwear in the family linen bin when his seven-year-old brother never has any accidents at all? Some DCD adolescents will even hide dirty under-wear somewhere private until they can wash it out themselves, usually in the middle of the night. Parents, getting cross or exasperated with your son or daughter won't solve this problem – they're already embarrassed enough.

Wet wipes are easier to use than toilet paper as they give you a larger surface area to grip. Their smell hides accidents. Take a packet of wipes out with you in case you need them, and try and establish a toilet routine. I know you can't go to the toilet on command (unless you are my superhuman mother, the woman who once restrained herself for a week when she was on a canal boat) but eating regular meals with plenty of roughage (sounds like a horse's diet – translates as: apples) can help.

Somehow I never envisaged myself having to write about poo…

Male health needs

I can't really comment on male health needs because as the more observant among you may have noticed, I'm not a male, so I had to turn to a group of boys with DCD in order to write this. They say that shaving is their biggest problem, and I can see that a razor blade is another of those many objects that doesn't go hand-in-hand with dyspraxia.

Electric shavers are apparently easier to use and are much safer. If you don't want one of these, buy razors with guards. Shave in a good light in front of a magnifying mirror and sit down while you do it. Check your face in a mirror before you leave the house, or you will end up casually strolling down the street with half your face unshaven. Be cautious with aftershave as you don't want to put too much on accidentally and smell as if you've been for a swim in the stuff.

Speaking of smells, another problem that teenage boys seem to have is keeping their body odour under control. This definitely isn't a problem unique to dyspraxic people. There is a group of lads at my school who neither have DCD or, it would appear, a bathtub in their houses. Perhaps this is just my hypersensitive dyspraxic nose talking, but I think not. You can avoid this effect by showering daily, using good shower gel and deodorant, and paying attention to your feet and armpits.

Female health needs

Looking after yourself during your period takes a lot of body awareness. Pick out the products that don't require so much co-ordination – stick-on pads (minus wings) are best to start with. Tampons are not a good option if you have fine-motor problems, and when you are at school or in a public toilet you might not have time to make sure that you are stable enough to use them. But if you swim or are really active then you may want to learn. Work out which type is easiest for you – applicator or non-applicator – and try putting them in with your knees bent in a slight squat. You may find it easier to insert them while sitting on the floor, or with one foot on the toilet seat. If you have poor body awareness then set a timer on your wristwatch or mobile to remind you to check yourself every two or three hours.

Some girls with DCD are so worried about getting into a mess that they check themselves compulsively every thirty minutes and carry half a pharmacy with them everywhere they go. If you do this you may as well pin a sign to your back announcing that you have your period! I know that you already have a lot to cope with at this time, but try to be as discreet as possible. Always carry sanitary pads and spare underwear in a small emergency bag tucked at the bottom of your schoolbag. Note the day that your period begins with a small tick in your appointment diary. This will remind you to prepare each month, so you're less likely to have an accident.

If you want to shave your legs, choose an electric shaver or one with a guard. You could also get someone to wax your legs for you, but don't try this if you have sensory problems or an unusually low pain tolerance! Depilatory cream is probably the best choice. It may be sloppy but it doesn't rip ribbons out of your kneecaps.

Personal appearance

Hairstyles

Your hair frames your face and alters the way your face looks, so it's important to strike a balance between flattering and easy to manage. Boys shouldn't let their hair grow too long and floppy otherwise it will be uncontrollable. It's also not a good idea to shave your head closely. This is an antisocial haircut and it will give future teachers or employers the wrong idea about you. But hair-brushing can be painful, and you'll have to find a length that doesn't look too messy when uncombed and yet isn't short enough to make you look like a die-hard member of a neo-Nazi movement! Don't try to elaborately style your hair if your fine-motor control isn't up to it, as you will look as if a miniature bush has just erupted from your scalp.

A bob or other short hairstyle is definitely the easiest choice for girls. If you have perceptual difficulties then using a mirror will be tricky so don't choose styles that require you to spend hours in front of the glass. Hair has a tendency to be selfishly unmanageable when you're in a hurry, so smoothening serum is useful. If you want long hair, ignore all the fiddly gadgets that are bursting out all over the shops like measles. Scrunchies and headbands are easy to put in and they're available in every colour. As your fine-motor control improves, try using chunky hair clips to scoop up all or part of your hair. A brush with a round, fat handle helps.

War paint

Makeup is a matter of life and death for many girls. I was once out shopping with someone who had no eyeliner on, and this meant that we had to dive for cover in shop doorways whenever we spotted anyone we knew. You will never catch me cowering behind the Woolworth's sweet counter just because I have no war paint on, but it does feel good when you know that you've done a great job on your eyes. If you can't see instinctively what looks right, ask someone to help.

- Forget about foundation. It is tricky to use (unevenly applied foundation looks awful) and it clogs up your pores. Concentrate instead on eyes and lips.

- Pick colours that match your eyes and skin tone rather than trying to colour co-ordinate your eye makeup with your clothes – mistakes are less noticeable this way.

- Some people find that it's easier to apply eye makeup with long-handled brushes. Others prefer to use their fingers.

- You can get eye shadow in the form of a giant crayon, which you simply rub on your eyelids. This is easier than using the powdered stuff or eyeliner.

- Mascara is tricky – you don't want black sticky stuff all over your eyeball. Consider getting your eyelashes dyed if you like the look of mascara. This has to be done once every six weeks.

- Coloured lip-glosses that you apply with fingers are better than lipsticks.

- If you want to use rouge, you can buy roll-on sticks that you run lightly over your cheekbones. It's less hassle than a brush and fine powder, as this ends up all over your shoulders and makes you look like you have pink dandruff.

- Nail varnishes are deadly and you're likely to end up with African tribal designs all over your fingers, so you should conscript a friend or sibling for nail-painting duty. If you want to try painting your own nails, choose a pale polish to start with as bright colours will gleefully show up your every slip.

- When you apply makeup, balance yourself in front of a magnifying mirror with plenty of light. Rest your elbow on a flat, stable surface as you work on your face to stop your hand slipping.

- The Japanese geisha look isn't popular outside the teahouses of Kyoto. The more war paint you use, the more obvious mistakes will be.

- Eyebrow plucking is tricky. Use a magnifying mirror to help (don't worry – they reveal spots that don't exist in real life) and don't try to shape your brows unless you have utmost confidence in your fine-motor skills. I doubt you do, considering that you've bought this book. Tidy up the straggling hairs and get someone else to do the shaping. (Warning: it seems to hurt more when other people do it for you!)

Glasses and contact lenses

Contact lenses take hours of practice but they're worth the effort. Soft monthly disposables are easier to adjust to than hard gas permeable ones. If you want to wear contacts, learn to put them in during a holiday. You will then return to school with your new 'face' and this could boost your self-esteem. If you can't manage contacts then select glasses that flatter your face shape.

Darker shades of dyspraxia

Adolescence is seething with changes – physical, social, educational, and emotional – and change is the one thing that makes your thoughts freeze and your hands go clammy. Without a strong routine to keep me anchored firmly to the ground, I lose my grip on the earth and go spinning off into the stratosphere. Now the professionals are starting to sift through the darker shades of the autistic spectrum, hoping to find reasons for the special problems that a lot of kids with learning difficulties go on to develop during adolescence. They have uncovered links between dyspraxia and depression and dyspraxia and low self-esteem. There may even be a slim thread connecting DCD to eating disorders such as anorexia nervosa and compulsive overeating.

I don't believe for one moment that having DCD makes you neurologically prone to these problems. I may not have a smart leather attaché case and a string of impressive-looking initials after my name, but this doesn't make any difference – I am telling it like it is from the inside, so my perception has got to be of value.

'Perception' is the key word in that sentence. Living with dyspraxia is like walking through a hall of mirrors. Your reflection is horrifically distorted, but it's hard for you to admit that you are not seeing a true representation of yourself – especially when you are surrounded by skewed definitions of disability and twisted ideas on what it means to be successful. For a lot of teenagers with DCD, it isn't just their spatial perception that's shaky.

House of mirrors?

I feel intelligent and stupid at the same time.

Joseph, 13

I have a brother and a sister who are good at almost everything. My brother is at university studying to become a lawyer and my sister wants to be a ballet dancer when she grows up. I'll never be like them, just look at how messy my writing is.

Priya, 12

I have a really hot temper and I'm frustrated when I can't
manage to do the stuff I want to do. I can't wait to get out of
school. It's pointless.

Paul, 13

I do get angry and annoyed sometimes. Doesn't everyone? But
it got a bit easier when I found out that I had dyspraxia and
dyslexia, and it's not because I'm not clever. So long as I keep
reminding myself of that, I'm all right.

Christopher, 15

Over to the dark side

For a long time I was haunted by the idea that there was something
wrong with me. This was the aftermath of bullying, and in many ways
the legacy was worse than the actual event. Whenever my mum and
dad and I ate at a restaurant, I refused to order my own food. I still
don't like talking to shop assistants or telephone operators or train-
ticket sellers or anyone whom I don't know. Even a friendly 'hello' is
pushing it. I also refuse to go anywhere without a thinking stick (a
pencil) in my hand. This must be either unsharpened or with a
razor-like lead. I don't like them if they are blunt. Its paint must not be
flaky and it should have a rubber at the top. The book and pencil
obsessions are 'problems' that I am very reluctant to cure myself of.
They're too useful.

Opening a book is like closing a solid oak door that shuts out the
noise and the confusing frustrations of the place on the other side. I
immerse myself so completely in the sights, sounds, smells, and tastes
of the story that my sensory problems are overridden – I once serenely
read through the unbearable wail of the school fire alarm simply
because my ears were on another planet. The key-keepers of Colditz
decided that they couldn't allow me to continue to go about with all
the tact, subtlety, and social adroitness of a flying dustbin lid, so they
gradually prised me away from the pages until I could walk through
the common room without my heart flapping about like a pigeon
on LSD.

At least my form of escapism was safe. For many others it is not. I can't excuse disruptive behaviour, but I can understand it. If I had been born with dyslexia in addition to a co-ordination disorder, what refuge would I have had then? I think I would have gone wild.

Coping with anger

Even someone as...um...positive and witty and shiningly optimistic as me gets fed up some of the time! As you may have noticed, my social skills are far from perfect and, despite my newfound confidence, I still sometimes feel the telltale anger curdling in my blood and fizzing through my veins.

I get angry when I spend ten minutes trying to steer my legs into my tights, only to end up ripping them. I get angry when I slop a cup of tea over an essay that took me hours to write. I get angry when people question how hard I try. ('You shouldn't have got the same effort grade as me – you always hand in your homework late, and mine is always on time.') I stutter with embarrassment when I miswrite someone's telephone number and end up dialling the Little Sisters of the Poor. This type of thing is funny once, or even twice, but with us it happens too much. Do any of you ever feel like shrieking at your body, 'For once in your life, just LISTEN TO ME!'?

The first thing you must do is to accept that none of this is your fault. It is, however, your responsibility. You need to devise your own personal anger-buster, whether it is punching a pillow or doing mad dancing to Urdu rock music. Try not to take your feelings out on other people, no matter how much they upset you. If someone doesn't seem to understand how annoyed and frustrated you are, try to explain as calmly as you can. Remember that it is OK to be angry, but you must be in control of the anger – never the other way round. It does take time to learn how to relax and to respond to your feelings in a quieter way, so you must make sure that you give yourself that time. Knowing the theory is always easier than putting it into practice!

You may feel as if you've had enough of coping by now. You may be bored with therapy, refuse even to consider new techniques to help with school, and hate the idea of taking up new hobbies. Someone who thinks like this might be tempted to brush off the things I have written here as airy-fairy junk. The only encouragement I can offer comes from my assessment report. I have severe dyspraxia (my performance skills place me in the bottom 0.3 per cent of the sixteen-year-old population) and while this is hardly a statistic to be proud of, it does show that I'm not underestimating how difficult things can get. I know that you may run out of mental petrol and get stuck in a rut, because I have been there myself. Trivial as it may sound, the best advice is – keep going. Life can get tiring and upsetting at times, but if you refuse to keep trying it will only stagnate around you.

Raising self-esteem

> What a smile!…it was the effluence of fine intellect, of true courage; it lit up her marked lineaments, her thin face, her sunken grey eye, like a reflection from the aspect of an angel. Yet at that moment Helen Burns wore upon her arm 'the untidy badge'; scarcely an hour ago I had heard her condemned to a dinner of bread and water on the morrow because she had blotted an exercise in copying it out. Such is the imperfect nature of man! Such spots are there on the disc of the clearest planet; and eyes like Miss Scatcherd's can only see these minute defects, and are blind to the full brightness of the orb.
>
> *Charlotte Brontë,* Jane Eyre

I have a beautiful velvet book in which I record my achievements – not just exam passes and certificates, but little things that make me proud of myself. Walking in a crowd without panicking. Eating neatly. Maintaining eye contact throughout a conversation. I like to flick through the book on grey days and remind myself of what I can do when I put my mind to it. You could do a similar thing. As a dyspraxic person, you have an original way of thinking that is very special and that many people will welcome.

I now try to take pride in my achievements – however small they may seem to others – as they take time, effort, and laborious practice.

Having this disability has taught me how to see the value in small things. It also means that I take nothing for granted. Thanks to our dyspraxia, we also have a lot of really cool gifts that might not be here if we were 'regular'. It is up to us to make the most of what we have. I see no reason for us to allow the things that we cannot do affect the things we can.

The obstacles that a dyspraxic person faces are often placed there by other people; not just by bullying bigots, but by their closest friends, who are trying to be helpful when they say, 'You won't be able to cope with that'. This is very muddling and it dazes me. By trying very hard at something or developing a particular skill, you will be gently teaching the people who care about you what it really means to have dyspraxia. In the end, the decision on whether you have a 'disability' or a 'difference' is yours and yours alone.

> I like people to ask if I need help first – before they start trying to help me, because I might just be doing it a different way and not needing help right then. I'll ask for help if I need it.
>
> *Tom, 12*

CHAPTER 9

Diagnosis – A Pipe Dream?

Make it thy business to know thyself, which is the most difficult
lesson in the world.

Miguel de Cervantes, Don Quixote

When I was diagnosed last year with dyspraxia, it changed my
life. Finally I had answers to the questions I had had for so long.
Why am I not like everybody else at school? Why do I have
messy handwriting? Why am I no good at catching things? The
list goes on.

Shaun, 17

Knowing me, knowing you

Not everyone is diagnosed in primary school. This is for all of you who
were like me and somehow slipped through the holes in the net. If you
have read through these pages with dawning comprehension, inwardly shouting, 'That's me!' you should seriously consider arranging
an assessment. It might help to make school fairer for you. If you have
to sit important exams without any help you will be at an awkward dis-
advantage. Some dyspraxic students are clever enough to get through

the exams with brain power and hard work, but the good or average grades that they earn through fatiguing revision could be better if they sat the exams on fair terms. Best of all, you will finally understand why you have felt different throughout your life.

For a teenager there are three routes to diagnosis. You can arrange an assessment with a psychologist through the special needs department at your college; you can go to your doctor and ask for a referral to the right professional; or you can refer yourself to a private occupational therapist or psychologist. After the initial assessment you might have to go and see someone else for a second evaluation. When I was assessed by the educational psychologist, she was amazed at me and sent me off to a neurologist to check that I wasn't brain-damaged. So began a game of pass-the-parcel. The neurologist sent me to an ophthalmologist and then to an occupational therapist, who has joined in the fun and referred me to a physio! Having so many tests carried out makes me feel a bit like an amoeba under a microscope, but I accept them good-naturedly – they are logical and have a purpose, even though that purpose (to get me some treatment) appears to be forty years into the future!

You may already be taking support lessons to help you with your work. If not, you need to approach the special needs teacher as soon as possible. Don't think that simply because you haven't been given extra help so far you can't have a problem. Many schools, including my own, seem to have dyspraxia themselves. The special needs department is a limb that has only recently begun to work in tandem with the rest of the school. Teachers are not always sure of their ground when it comes to learning difficulties and they are ridiculously wary of getting involved with them.

The lady who assessed me was incredibly shocked that I had somehow managed to stumble through fifteen years of my life without anyone picking up on the severity of my problems. Being eloquent and articulate actually did me a disservice here. My strengths threw a confusing smokescreen over the glaring reality of my handicap, especially during the primary school years. After all, how many ten-year-olds read Jane Austen? But the smokescreen started to dissolve as soon as I walked through the doors of my first secondary school. Secondary schools are places of turbulent change, and change has always spelled out defeat for me. I had fewer routines to cling to at a time when I needed routine more than ever before. I was playing a dangerous game of cat-and-mouse with the nameless strangeness. And if I hadn't got my label, there is no doubt about who would have won.

To this day, many people persist in believing that no bright kid can possibly have difficulties. 'You get extra time in exams? But I thought you were quite clever!' one lad once said to me, obviously really puzzled. When I explained that any gifts I had were because of my dyspraxia, not in spite of it, I think I bewildered him even more. It's not just other teenagers who get muddled by this concept, but some teachers. I speak from the bowels of experience (not a great place to be!) when I say that it is very difficult for a person with dyspraxia, no matter how intelligent they may be, to live up to expectations when they have no extra support. This is why diagnosis is so vital.

Go to the special needs teacher and ask to discuss your difficulties with them. Unless your form tutor is useless and/or a bully, you should try and involve them too, otherwise they might end up miffed that they were left out of things. Your special teacher will be able to call in the right professional to perform an assessment. Theoretically, assessment should be free. (Yes, the 't' word!) We had to pay for mine because the psychologist who liaises with my school doesn't work for the local education authority or the NHS.

If your school has no special needs department (or is unwilling to arrange an assessment) go to your GP. You should have the following information as backup:

- A list of DCD-connected problems that you feel you suffer from. You could write to the Dyspraxia Foundation or visit their website for this.

- The name of someone who knows about dyspraxia at your local hospital. (The Dyspraxia Foundation will help you to pinpoint appropriate contacts.)

- A friend or parent to support you.

- A polite and committed attitude. Try saying something like, 'I've got problems that affect my learning and daily living. I think dyspraxia is the cause and I'd like to see a specialist who could assess me for it'.

- Emphasize that you really do need help. Implying that all you want is a label and an official 'I have dyspraxia' stamp won't go down well.

Your third option is private diagnosis. If you contact the Dyspraxia Foundation, the Dyscovery Centre, the British Dyslexia Association, or the Dyslexia Institute (lots of choice!) they will be able to help you find a professional in your area who conducts assessments for learning difficulties, but you will have to pay a fee. Private assessments are not cheap.

What happens at the assessment?

> For the first time in my life I was told that it is OK to be different. It was so cool to hear that!
>
> *Paul, 13*

'Vicky, you look so white!' Mrs A exclaimed when she came into the Learning Support room on the day of my assessment.

The Assessment. Bang.

'You don't have to go through with it, you know,' she whispered.

I knew that my support teacher hadn't slept much the night before. Mrs A had told me that she always lies awake the night before one of her students is due to be assessed, panicking on their behalf. Why were we both so worried? I didn't know. It wasn't as if I were going to have major surgery. I was going to find out, once and for all, whether I had a learning difference or whether I was just like everybody else. But there I was, the colour of anaemic chalk, fighting to keep my breakfast down.

I walked out of the room three hours later feeling dazed, upset, and very happy at the same time. Mrs A, who hadn't stayed for the assessment, came rushing to meet me. 'Well?' she said. 'I'm dyspraxic,' I replied, and my voice seemed to come from a thousand miles away.

'Oh, Vicky, we *knew* that,' she said softly, and hugged me. Even though she was wearing a scratchy coat that felt horrible against my face, I hugged her back. Yes, I had known that I had a learning difficulty called dyspraxia from the moment I first saw the word. But I still needed the assessment – not just to get the right help, but to reassure me that I had a genuine difficulty and wasn't just 'weird'. Isn't it amazing when, after you've been labelled 'freak' for so long, you learn that you aren't one?

So why was I scared of that assessment? Looking back, I think I was afraid of failure. I didn't want to sit down in front of a test paper that I couldn't do. I'd had enough of that type of thing. But once the assessment began I realized that it wasn't a graded test. There are no right or wrong answers.

People under sixteen will normally be assessed using the Wechsler Intelligence Scales for Children (WISC). Those of you who are sixteen and over will be assessed with the Wechsler Adult Intelligence Scales (WAIS). The adult assessment isn't radically different from the one designed for children. The format is just a little different.

The assessment is divided into two portions, verbal and performance. Remember that any learning difficulties that you may have don't affect your overall intelligence. The assessor uses an IQ test to work out whether your ability to do certain tasks matches your level of intelligence. If there is a big discrepancy, there is a possibility that you have learning difficulties.

There are eleven subtests in the assessment. Six of them are verbal and five are performance-based. The verbal section includes word definition tests, general knowledge questions, and the repetition of lists of digits forwards and backwards. Your reading, spelling, comprehension, arithmetic and memory skills are assessed in this section. The performance section consists of tasks that are not based on language, such as using a numerical key to find and copy symbols and constructing a three-dimensional jigsaw with red and white blocks. You will be given a set of pictures and asked to arrange them in the correct sequence so that they tell a story. You will be asked to look at a set of drawings and try to spot what is strange about the pictures. Often there is a set of physical tests – balancing on one leg, jumping and hopping, kicking a ball and performing a finger tapping sequence. You might have to write something out so that the assessor can see what your handwriting is like.

The assessment yields three scores – a verbal quotient, a performance quotient, and a full-scale IQ score. A significant gap between your verbal and performance skills is one of the classic indicators of developmental dyspraxia. There is a discrepancy the size of the Grand Canyon between mine. My verbal skills place me in the ninety-ninth percentile and my performance skills (or my lack of them) put me in the first percentile. The results of your assessment are plotted on graphs and you are told what the averages for other people your age are and if you differ from those. The psychologist will then write out a full report of what they've found out.

Some people mistakenly think that having an assessment is like getting diagnosed with a terrible disease. I did have to have a brain scan and a blood test and all sorts of things after my clinical psychologist Carys diagnosed me with dyspraxia, just to check that the problem really was developmental and I didn't have brain damage or a chromosomal abnormality such as Fragile X. These extra tests don't usually come up with anything you don't already know. Biologically based co-ordination problems are very rare, especially in girls.

Some young people with dyspraxia are happy to go on without a professional's letter. For them, their own self-diagnosis is enough; a psychologist could offer them nothing more than they have already. If this is you, don't feel like you have to get an assessment. It is an option that is there only if you need exam concessions, or if 'knowing for sure' would make you feel better about yourself.

> While I was at college, when I was eighteen, my mum found an article from a Guide magazine. It was about a Guide who was dyspraxic. She wrote about what she found difficult in everyday life. Mum showed it to me and said, 'That's you'. I immediately agreed and we decided that that's what I had. No need to go to a psychologist, it was there in black and white.
>
> *Abby, 19*

When silence is deadly

I am a person who always needs to 'know for sure' to feel confident. I often wondered why I seemed to think and work differently from other children my age, and I went through my first three years of secondary school feeling like the proverbial sore thumb. It was only when I made my first friend at Colditz that I began to put two and two together. Emma is dyslexic. Emma is very like me. Could I possibly be…?

I was surfing the Internet for information on dyslexia when I accidentally wandered into Matt's Hideout, a website that announced in bold type, 'I dedicate this website to sufferers of dyspraxia all over the world'. The creator of the site is a fourteen-year-old boy who can't pour juice into a cup, tie his shoelaces, follow complicated instructions or organize either his environment or the inside of his head. As I read through the symptoms of Developmental Co-ordination Disorder I realized that I was looking into a mirror. A tidal wave of sheer relief washed over me, followed by something that can only be described as ecstasy. I immediately headed into town and ordered a book on specific learning difficulties. Once I had read it from cover to cover, I approached one of the key-keepers of Colditz, brimming over with information and excitement.

'Mrs S, I've been reading this book and I think I have dyspraxia.'

She laughed gently. 'Tell me something I didn't know.'

Excuse me?!

She had apparently picked up on my problems within a week of my arrival at Colditz. 'Don't you remember how I once asked you to line up your books in neat piles, and to try and fasten a blouse?'

Yes, I remembered. But that had been three years ago. Why hadn't she said anything to me then, instead of allowing me to go daily into a classroom where a group of kids with IQs below room temperature had been making my life so difficult?

She explained that some parents dislike the suggestion that their child is less than 100 per cent perfect, and that my mum and dad might have been angry with her if she had attached a label to me. I understand that some parents are probably like this, but when a child's education and quite possibly his sense of self-worth is at stake, I think that teachers ought to take the risk. It turned out that our next-door neighbour in Saudi Arabia had also recognized dyspraxia in me, as had a lady who goes to the dancing class that my half-sister teaches, as had my autistic nephew's support worker. I was somewhat annoyed that half the population seemed to know about my special needs before I stumbled across them myself, and I think that if anyone in a position of authority over a child – a parent, a teacher, or a close family friend – suspects that he or she has DCD, they should immediately persuade the parents to give the news.

Mrs S quietly provided a lot of support for me in the days before I discovered the nature of my difference. She always 'happened to be passing by' my room when I had to tidy up or pack and she never pressed me to go and sit in a noisy common room with a bunch of peculiar people. But even though I trusted her, sensing that she understood a bit about the way I thought, I wasn't able to understand myself.

Knowing about dyspraxia comes as a great relief after years of self-doubt and pretending to be normal – at least, it does to most people. I understand that there are some teenagers who see it as a weakness and so try to ignore their own brain. For me, getting a diagnosis felt like the sun coming out after a cold day of rain. Keeping a learning difference secret suggests that it is something to be ashamed of, and even though

I understand Mrs S's reasons for staying silent, I don't think that any adolescent with dyspraxia needs to be burdened with the belief that they are freakish or abnormal. Unnecessary secrecy is just one more padlock on the cage.

Why am I different?

Occasionally I come across people who think that if I sneeze they'll catch my 'disease'. This is impossible because dyspraxia isn't a virus. The reason for it is buried in the most mysterious organ of the human body. The cause? Most scientists agree that the neurones in the dyspraxic brain have developed differently from other people's.

Imagine a fishing-net pulled tight over a human brain. The cords are the neural pathways and the knots where the cords intertwine are the synapses. When we try to learn something the information shoots along these pathways until it comes to a synapse, which is like a chasm that needs to be bridged before the information can enter our memory. With most people these bridges are built within milliseconds, but the dyspraxic mind can't always construct them. The information tumbles headlong into the chasm and is lost.

> Having dyspraxia feels like there are too many thoughts in your head, like too many cars trying to get the wrong way down a one-way street.
>
> *Joel, 14*

There are truckloads of different theories as to why we are like this. *Guide to Dyspraxia and Developmental Co-ordination Disorders* (Kirby and Drew 2002) outlines several very convincing ones, but as the brain is so vast and complicated it's impossible to pick out one common cause. It's likely that there is not just one cause, but several, and these may even differ from person to person. The autistic spectrum is like a recipe book with missing pages and blurred handwriting that make the recipes hard to follow. No one knows exactly what ingredients produce a child with learning differences.

The brain has two hemispheres, which are responsible for different things. The left hemisphere deals with language, logic, and analytical thinking. It is also associated with feelings of happiness. The right hemisphere controls spatial awareness, visual and touch sensations, co-ordination and lateral thinking. This is also the part of the brain that helps us to understand emotions and humour.

Teenagers with DCD tend to be weak at tasks involving the right hemisphere and are better with left-brained activities. (If you have the typical dyspraxic problems with laterality all these lefts and rights will be hell for you to sort out – sorry about that!) This is not brain damage. When a person with dyspraxia goes for a brain scan there is no sign of abnormality, backing up the idea that DCD is a result of immature neurones.

Researchers are trying to work out whether smoking, drinking, drug abuse or an expectant mother's diet is responsible for causing neurological differences in an unborn child. There is a learning difference called DAMP, a cocktail of attention and motor perception deficits, which seems to be linked to maternal smoking. This area of study is still wobbly, but the possibility is there.

There is definitely a correlation between learning difficulties and premature birth. I was born at thirty weeks and the neurologist suggested that I might be dyspraxic because of that. Many children who attend special needs support centres were born too early or too late. There also seems to be a link between DCD and glue ear. If you suffered from this when you were little it could have magnified existing co-ordination problems and caused your difficulties to deepen into an actual disorder. Then again, glue ear could be a result of the co-ordination disorder and not the other way round – little kids with dyspraxia might not be able to drain their ears as well as other children.

Now that I've put everyone off their next meal with that delightful thought, I will talk a bit about food! It's unlikely that a bad diet causes learning difficulties; it probably just irritates the symptoms. There are lots of supplements and special diets – the Feingold programme (www.feingold.org) is probably the most famous – that are recommended for people with dyspraxic difficulties. There does seem to be a connection between DCD and a lack of essential fatty acids (EFAs) which can be got from eating fish and taking supplements. These are good for the brain's development. I know that some parents are very irresponsible about nourishing their kids, just banging down chips and easy-cook pizzas in front of them, so perhaps primary schools should start providing breakfast clubs and secondary schools should offer healthy school dinners. Our canteen is swimming in chip fat, which isn't exactly the best fuel for brains that are about to be saturated in exams.

One of my favourite Arab sayings is 'the son of a duck is a floater'. Before you all start thinking strange things about my taste in language I will hastily explain that the proverb's real meaning is 'like father, like son', and has nothing to do with the contents of a toilet. In some cases there is a thread of disabilities running through a family and if one of your parents is also dyspraxic, or has a similar condition like dyslexia, it is possible that you inherited your gift from them.

There is a streak of autism in my family, and perhaps dyslexia as well. My brother has never been formally assessed, but he is skilled at all the things I'm not. He's a very practical person – good at sport and a brilliant chef. But his letters to me are riddled with punctuation errors and he isn't too sure about which way the tail of the letter 'g' should face. He sometimes mixes up the order of words too. These aren't just ordinary spelling errors. I have a dyslexic friend in school who does exactly the same sort of thing.

I think my mum might be mildly dyspraxic because she has the memory of a squirrel and she is always late for things. If there is anything that can be tripped over, you can be pretty sure that she will trip over it (normally breaking a few toes along the way) and like me she has no aptitude for numbers. But she was the star of my old school's parents' netball team and she's a little too well organized for my flamboyant taste. She can home in on a stray sock or a few scattered books like sensitive radar and we sometimes have interesting 'discussions' on what is tidy, so maybe not!

The most important thing to take from all this information, even more important than reasons or origins, is that while your unique neurology may cause you to short-circuit from time to time, it's also capable of generating some great ideas. And even though having dyspraxia doesn't automatically make you a genius, it's comforting to know that it's no guarantee of lack of intelligence either. The knowledge that people like Einstein were also caged in this mad chaos has pulled me through many a bad day.

> Remember, everyone's different, and we should celebrate these differences because it's what makes each of us special. Dyspraxia has made me the person I am, and in a way, I'm happy about that.
>
> *Matthew, 14*

Sticky labels

One reason why people resist diagnosis is because they feel that once they are labelled they'll never be able to shake off the implications of that label. Some argue that everyone should just be accepted for what they are and receive help catered to their specific needs without any further questions being asked. Should we throw out all labels altogether?

I personally think that this would be a pretty stupid thing to do. Imagine going into a supermarket and finding that all the labels had been removed from tins and packets. How would you know which food was which, where to find what you wanted, how to check the ingredients? Or, as I prefer to think of the word 'dyspraxia' as a signpost rather than a label, a better analogy might be to imagine a city stripped of all its road signs. The labels are necessary legally because they help professionals to differentiate between people who really need specialized help and those who could catch up with a little extra coaching. Kids are more likely to get help if a teacher knows that they have a specific problem area. Otherwise it could just be shrugged off as laziness on the part of the pupil – and I have had way too much of that treatment in my time!

Parents and carers often feel much better for receiving a diagnosis. It is a sad fact that many parents would prefer a diagnosis of Scatty-Batty Syndrome than nothing at all. When things seem to go wrong, there always has to be a reason, an answer, an excuse – anything to relieve the worry and the upset. But while dyspraxia is the reason, and diagnosis an answer, there is no excuse lurking behind a psychologist's report. Being officially diagnosed does not mean that either the parents or the dyspraxic person can throw up their hands and give up.

Dyspraxia is virtually unheard of in some communities. If you are a doctor who has never heard of DCD then you obviously cannot diagnose it. It's the same for all differences on the spectrum. Dyspraxic people are frequently misdiagnosed as dyslexic in countries where DCD is little known. Should the diagnostic criteria be internationally standardized? If learning differences are truly developmental then they will be the same across all cultures, and the same labels can be applied.

But although dyspraxia is the same condition in Britain as it is in Pakistan, the two cultures are so different that standardized criteria might be difficult to use. My best friend Sobia is Pakistani. I love going to her house because when we eat, we often sit on the floor and use our fingers to scoop up food. This is normal in Asian houses and it's a very dyspraxia-friendly way of eating – I never feel the same panic and sense of doom that I get when I'm forced to be a guest in an English house. And in Arab sitting rooms you won't always find chairs; Saudis like to sit on the floor, leaning on cushions. It would be much harder to spot dyspraxic teenagers in these countries because the culture camouflages the fundamental co-ordination and balance problems.

The same is true of other specific difficulties. In China the language is written in pictures. Many foreigners learn to read the picture characters but they can't speak the language because speaking and reading are disconnected. There must surely be dyslexia in China, because it affects more than the ability to write and spell, but as the picture-writing system fits in so well with the dyslexic mindset it will be harder for teachers to detect students with this problem. This is why it is probably better to use different diagnostic criteria from country to country, so it seems to me, as no one can be neatly squashed into a doctor's checklist.

I am frequently referred to as a 'classic dyspraxic', a label that makes me feel a bit like an ancient car in a transport museum, but in reality there is no such thing as the textbook DCD adolescent. We are many vivid variations on the same theme, and the professionals who dish out the labels should take this into account.

What does it mean to have...
AUTISM?

This is a really complex and mysterious area that deserves a whole book to itself, and my knowledge of it comes from my nephew. Autistic people are generally described as having a triad of impairments in communication, social interaction, and imagination. The last point can be a bit confusing. This doesn't necessarily mean that autistics aren't creative, but that they have difficulty imagining alternative outcomes to different situations and events. They tend to take language very literally and have sensory problems too.

Low-functioning autistic people may not want to talk at all. They are locked into their own world of obsessions, compulsions, and rigid repetitive behaviours. Ben used to be obsessed with the bezel on my dad's watch and would sit twisting it round and round for hours. Although from our perspective a life like this might look bleak, we have no knowledge of what the world is like from the eyes of someone like Ben. Maybe fiddling with a wristwatch is as wonderful and exciting to him as going out to a nightclub is to others. Both activities seem pretty strange to me, but I can't judge. (Not while pencil-flicking still features on my list of favourite activities, anyway!)

High-functioning autistic people are very different. They interact with the world around them, although they do it in their own unique way. An example of a very successful person with HFA is Dr Temple Grandin. She has loads of qualifications in agriculture and has written several books about her experiences – try *Thinking in Pictures and Other Reports of My Life With Autism* (1996).

ASPERGER SYNDROME?

This is a variation on high-functioning autism. Teenagers with Asperger's are frequently described as being 'mildly autistic'. I don't know anyone with AS who would call their problem 'mild'; the one person I know has a difficult time of it at school, especially with socializing and understanding aspects of language. Unfortunately the syndrome is often explained away as the result of childhood trauma, a sudden change to the teenager's life, a death in the family, or something like that. Bill Gates, the director of Microsoft, is thought to have this because of his strong need for routine and his obsessive, repetitive behaviours. The Asperger diagnosis makes sense as the logic demanded by computing is often part of an AS person's character – this is why it is sometimes nicknamed 'the engineers' disorder'.

HYPERLEXIA?

This is the precocious, self-taught ability to read fluently and speedily at an early age. Hyperlexic people have an intense fascination with words and numbers and usually have photographic memories. They have problems communicating with other people and making sense of non-verbal language, and socializing is difficult for them.

SEMANTIC-PRAGMATIC DISORDER?

This is a disorder that affects language and communication skills. A person with this problem would have a hard time understanding a term like, 'He cried his eyes out,' and might become upset at the thought of eyeballs being washed onto the floor! The interpretation of language is also affected. 'He is hot,' can mean, 'He is feeling the temperature,' but it can also mean, 'He's gorgeous'. How to make the distinction? People all over the spectrum seem to have this problem to some degree.

Those of you who lean towards this part of the spectrum might also have trouble categorizing things – for instance, how are the numbers nine and twenty-five alike? This was a question I got asked at my assessment. (When I asked my support teacher she said that they were both odd.)

ATTENTION DEFICIT/HYPERACTIVITY DISORDER?

Attention Deficit Disorder, with or without the hyperactivity, is the chronic inability to concentrate – even if you are interested in what is going on around you, even if you want to pay attention, your mind (and often your body!) roves off into another world. This can happen without the AD/HD person realizing it. 'Hang on, I didn't know I *wasn't* in my seat!'

DYSLEXIA?

Mainly a difficulty in learning to read, write, and spell, dyslexia affects all sorts of other stuff such as short-term memory and organization. It is very similar to dyspraxia here. Dyslexic people have the same left–right confusion problems, the same sense of disorientation when in a strange place, and difficulties with timekeeping and time management. As a teenager, a dyslexic person might muddle up instructions and still have problems with handwriting.

DYSCALCULIA?

This literally means 'difficulty with calculations'. People with dyscalculia have big problems with numbers, mathematical concepts, timekeeping, and perception. Some people are unable to look at a picture of a cube and see a solid shape. They logically reason that if it is on paper it's got to be flat. They also have difficulty with spatial concepts such as 'behind', 'beneath', and 'in front of'. This seems to be an extension of laterality problems, as dyslexic and dyspraxic children often struggle with the same thing.

Technically, the 'dyses' are not full-blooded autistic spectrum disorders. But they do seem to share a lot of traits with autism and most experts agree that all the above conditions are linked in some way, although some are obviously much more complex than others. I see the spectrum as a bit like a radio in this respect. Each difference carries its own wavelength and frequency, but the messages that are transmitted are very similar. If autism is a tree trunk, and Asperger Syndrome and the other pervasive developmental disorders its branches, then differences such as dyslexia and dyspraxia are its leaves and blossoms.

CHAPTER 10

Dealing with Dyspraxia: What Can I Do Now?

> Lord, grant me the serenity to accept the things I cannot change, the courage to change the things I can, and the wisdom to know the difference.
>
> *Reinhold Niebuhr,* The Serenity Prayer

Treatment and therapy

Dyspraxia is with you for life. For this reason I have tried to be very positive throughout this book, helping people with DCD to look for ways to cope rather than to go out searching for ways to cure. But some aspects of dyspraxia are very uncomfortable, so here is a summary of the different types of therapy available that will help you to deal with these facets of DCD. If you were diagnosed with another difference as well as dyspraxia, I'm sorry that I haven't offered much advice on coping with that. If I talked about all the learning difficulties there are we would have to pulverize the Amazon forest to get enough paper!

Focusing on the practical skills that dyspraxic individuals find hard to learn, occupational therapists hunt out gadgets and equipment that you may find useful. I have a set of moulded cutlery, a special chair in each classroom, and a huge collection of timers and electronic reminders. Occupational therapists can also put together exercise programmes to help you improve your perception and motor control. If your organization is a big problem, they may also work out some strategies to help you sort this out. I once saw a lady called Mrs Deuteronomy (well, that's what her surname sounded like) and we worked on my posture and fine-motor skills and movement. All the exercises she had were aimed at little children ('Pick up the zebra beanbag with your left hand!') as no one seems to have given much thought to teenagers and our needs yet. I wish they would, as I'd like to be able to do occupational therapy without the Pink Panther getting in on the act. As it is, a few hours of zebra beanbags is the sum total of my OT. Mrs Deuteronomy did give me some worksheets to help me improve my fine-motor control, but doing them was about as stimulating as watching paint dry and I stupidly tucked them away in a drawer to gather dust. These games and worksheets might have helped me when I was younger, but now I'm facing an adulthood spent in the company of dyspraxia I need more functional strategies to cope with aspects of daily living – how to cook a meal, how to use public transport safely. The nature of the therapy definitely has to change with the child.

Some dyspraxic teenagers suffer from sensory dysfunction. There is a specialized form of OT designed to retrain your brain to properly integrate and organize the information that comes crowding in through your senses. Sensory integration therapy is usually made up of a set of physical exercises, coupled with the use of equipment like spinning chairs and flashing lights. It can be useful for those of you who get frightened in sensory-intensive situations or otherwise feel that your senses overload you with information that you can't understand. My nephew goes to a special school for children with autism and they have a room fitted with lava lamps, glitter balls, and those illuminated columns that are filled with bubbling water. The floor is carpeted with lots of different textures. All the children with sensory problems can go there for structured therapy or just to mess around.

As the name suggests, physiotherapy concentrates on the physical problems that your body has as a result of DCD. A physiotherapist will work with you on your posture, balance, and muscle tone. This type of therapy focuses solely on you, not on making adjustments to your environment. I have recently started going to physiotherapy sessions. My gait already has a little more rhythm and, for the first time ever, my limbs feel as if they are working together. (I have just knocked over a friend's cup of tea and she is crossly insisting that she can see no difference, but I can!) I can't describe how amazing this sensation is. I haven't transformed into a graceful swan-like creature, but last week I nearly managed to open a tin of rice pudding by myself. That's fine for starters!

Do any of you have verbal dyspraxia, or at least some difficulty with the clarity of your speech? Jarrod Behan is a thirteen-year-old with these problems and he was bullied a lot because of the way he speaks. His therapist worked with him on enunciation and breath control and all the other things that you need to speak clearly. Like me, he goes to boarding school and his mum reports that he has been much more confident around other kids since his speech started to improve. The telling slogan for the speech and language association AFASIC (Association for Speech Impaired Children) is 'the limits of my language are the limits of my world'. It must be horribly frustrating to know what you want to say but not be able to get it out of your mouth.

Even if you don't have verbal dyspraxia, don't rule out speech therapy as a possibility. Speech therapists can help with non-verbal communication such as body language. They may also work with you on improving your social skills, so if you struggle to make sense of body language and don't mix very well, this could help you.

Complementary therapies

- T'ai Chi: this ancient Chinese Taoist discipline focuses on bringing you harmony and clarity of mind through a series of physical exercises. The exercises are not challenging and they have helped my co-ordination. If there are no T'ai Chi classes in your area then you can teach yourself out of books, such as *T'ai Chi, Chi Kung* by Peter Chin Kean Choy.

- Reflexology: this treatment works on the premise that doing certain things to your feet can affect your overall well-being. I'm a little sceptical about this – but maybe that's because I don't have the best feet in the world. They're the size of skis and have a very weird shape. They are definitely not indicative of the state of the rest of my body. I'm not in that much of a mess!

- Meditation: you don't have to sit cross-legged in an icy Himalayan cave to benefit from this. It is soothing, peaceful, and sharpens your concentration.

The miracle mackerel

The saying 'you are what you eat' is very true for adolescents with DCD. There is a strong correlation between dyspraxia and a lack of Essential Fatty Acids. Dr Jacqueline Stordy (2002) has published a book (*The LCP Solution: The Amazing Nutritional Treatment for Dyslexia, Dyspraxia, and AD/HD*) that talks about how to correct EFA deficiency through special diets and supplementation. The fish-oil supplements Eye-Q and Efalex have received a lot of good press lately and there is a towering pyramid of Eye-Q bottles in Boots, their labels promising improved concentration, co-ordination, short-term memory and all sorts of other things.

Encouraged by all the success stories, I tried myself on Eye-Q and…it didn't work. However, I do know many people with dyspraxia who have improved dramatically after a few months of supplementation. Why does the miracle mackerel work for some and not for others? There is no satisfactory explanation at the moment, but I have a sneaking suspicion that it could be to do with the subtle difference between dyspraxia and Developmental Co-ordination Disorder.

I have used the two terms pretty much interchangeably throughout this book, because the impact they have on teenage life is identical. But many doctors use the term 'dyspraxia' to indicate a specific difficulty with motor planning. The dyspraxic brain and nerve system have no idea how to co-ordinate your movements to allow you to pick up that kettle without slopping hot water everywhere. By contrast, the DCD brain knows exactly what it needs to do, but the messages get scrambled in transit and the body can't carry out the brain's instructions. It could be that fish oils have no effect on dyspraxic people, but a brilliant impact on those with DCD – or vice versa. It will be very difficult to find out if my theory is true, as the dividing line between dyspraxia and DCD is so blurred. There is only one real way to discover whether supplementation will work for you. You can but try!

Crushing the cage

I've written about all the different therapies 'available' (ha) as if they are incredibly easy to get hold of. In my area occupational therapists are rarer than gold dust and most physios are obsessed with sports injuries, sports injuries, and still more sports injuries. I believe that nearly all people with DCD really need professional help as there is only so much that you can do alone. Here I've included some of the things that fall into the 'so much' category. I haven't tried all of these activities myself (get real!) but each one has been recommended to me by either a dyspraxic person or someone involved with special needs.

My personal favourite is Arabic dance. I go to a class where the teacher is very supportive of my difficulties and the emphasis is more on keeping fit and having a laugh than becoming the next star of Cairo. I can hardly wait to get there each week, slip on my bell-studded anklets, and just dance. My muscles ache, I lose track of the sequences, confuse right and left, and yet I love it. In the Middle East, where I used to live, nobody is ever in a rush and there is no pressure to succeed now, at once, immediately. Arab culture is a dyspraxic dream – there, you always have plenty of time. This is the spirit that infuses the dance. No matter what hobby you choose, try to borrow this happy way of thinking. You need to find an activity that both accepts and absorbs you, and pour all your excess emotions into that. I can walk into the dance studio bubbling over with frustration, but all the hurts and hassles of the day soon dissolve beneath my pounding feet.

Therapy in disguise

'A KARATE STORY' BY MATTHEW, 14

I joined a karate class to try to help me with my co-ordination and stamina. Before I joined the club, my mum explained to the Senseis (teachers) that I had difficulty with my co-ordination, balance, and muscle strength, because of my dyspraxia. She asked if they would be happy for me to join their classes and they told her that they would be very happy for me to join the club.

When I first started, I was very good at it. It was fun and I enjoyed myself. I went through several gradings and loads of lessons. I worked very hard and was proud of my achievements. My mum continued to check my progress with the Senseis and they told her that I was doing well and keeping up with all the children. Then, when we got our orange belt, the lessons became harder and one-hour lessons became two hours long.

During the two-hour lessons I became tired and found the moves more difficult to do. That's when the problems started. My Senseis began to make fun of me in front of the class, mimicking my moves and saying things like, 'Look, the new downward block!' which made me feel upset, angry, and humiliated. I put up with it for a few weeks before I confided in my mum.

My mum questioned how I was being treated and reminded the Senseis I had dyspraxia. She was told I was lazy and that in their opinion, 'Being lazy was not a disability'. They then said that Clare and I were the poorest students in the class and would never pass our next grading, therefore our membership to the club had been cancelled. In actual fact, Clare was good at karate. I feel I was thrown out because they were being spiteful and Clare was thrown out for being my sister.

What made me feel so downcast when I read Matt's story is the fact that he was good at karate. If his teachers had been a bit more understanding he could have continued to do well. When you sign up for a sports club, take along a written explanation of dyspraxia so that the instructors know how to help you. Join small groups or classes so you will get more individual attention. And no matter how staggeringly daunting your chosen activity may seem at the beginning, keep working at it. One of the best things about DCD is that it teaches you to be extremely determined.

I know the very idea of volunteering to do extra sport must sound as if it has come from an insane brain, but if you have ever complained of being exhausted during the day, if you have ever wished that your legs didn't feel like jelly after walking uphill, if you've ever spent pounds on magical creams to banish spots, then doing some sport (not team sports, as I spend half my time working out ways to get out of these) is what you need.

Fun and games (yes, seriously!)

- Swimming is the best exercise there is. It uses all your muscles and helps with low tone, bilateral integration, and breath control, which is really good for people who have verbal dyspraxia.

- Yoga boosts muscle tone and balance and helps with flexibility, clearing the mind at the same time. It is also an integral part of Hindu religion. Although non-Hindus can practise it, you should approach it with respect. It shouldn't be treated like some clichéd celebrity fad. Out of the many different yoga types, Iyengar yoga is probably best for us. Its founder devised many aspects of it with disabled practitioners in mind.

- Horse-riding is good for balance, posture, rhythm, and strength. More importantly, the horse doesn't care whether you are purple with gold polka dots. This animal isn't going to judge you. There are even riding schools with special programmes for disabled riders.

- Rock-climbing benefits concentration, co-ordination, and muscle strength.

- Martial arts are good for co-ordination, stamina, and self-confidence. Pick a non-competitive club that doesn't have too many people in it, so that you can go at your own pace.

- Dancing is excellent for co-ordination, spatial awareness, balance, and concentration, but you should be careful which type you choose. The marked lack of dyspraxic dancers leaping around Covent Garden tells you that ballet might be a little difficult! Line dancing improves sequencing skills and there is always someone else to follow if you get lost, and in Arabic dance the emphasis is on strengthening the muscles and developing rhythm, not on co-ordination.

- Badminton is probably the most dyspraxic-friendly racquet sport. Try a synthetic shuttlecock rather than a feathered one as they are easier to hit.

- Canoeing, sailing and rowing can be done individually or in a team, so once you feel ready you can join a boating club – an opportunity to make new friends.

- Aqua-aerobics are a diluted version of ordinary aerobics. These may be too difficult but in the water the moves are slower and more fluid, while the benefit remains the same.

- Trampolining is brilliant for posture, balance, and flexibility. At my special teacher's suggestion I will be starting at a disabled class in a few weeks, so we'll see how this goes. (One of my old roommates is now demanding to know where she can get tickets. Wait one moment whilst we engage in a pillow fight.)

- Ice-skating is great for balance. Go to the rink when there aren't many people there if you are bad with crowds, and take someone with you to be your personal handrail. Check that loud music and bright lights aren't used if you suffer from poor sensory integration.

- Scuba diving is an unusual activity that improves muscle tone and concentration. I had the added boon of learning in the Red Sea...I wouldn't recommend it if you live off the Blackpool coast.

Helpful hobbies

- Pottery: working with pliable materials like clay is a good way to improve fine motor control.

- Chess: some teenagers with specific learning differences can become phenomenal chess players. It's good for your concentration, sequencing skills, and organization of thought. It isn't restricted to age, either – you and your opponents are matched according to skill level, so there is no pressure for you to improve at exactly the same speed as everyone else.

- Jenga is a great game to play. It really helps your fine-motor skills. You construct a tower out of wooden Jenga blocks and then try to dismantle it, bit by bit, without the tower toppling. It's more fun when you're having a competition within a group of people.

- Creative writing: let your imagination go.

- Music or art appreciation: these allow you to gain knowledge of culture that could be fed back into some of your lessons at school.

- Playing a musical instrument: don't worry about your proficiency level – I've been learning piano for seven years, and have yet to get past 'Ode to Joy' and 'Bobby Shaftoe'. I play because I love music. Choose an instrument that allows you to sit down to play for the sake of your balance.

- Art: fine pen-and-ink sketches and delicate brushwork may be too difficult, so you'll have to go with something less precise. At least your artwork will be funky and original!

- Photography: an outlet of artistic expression that doesn't require too much co-ordination. It helps to improve spatial awareness, as you have to think about the careful positioning of objects in the camera frame.

- Cookery: this helps you to develop concentration and sequencing skills. Plus, the results are of an edible variety…

- Drama: brilliant for self-confidence, communication skills, and body awareness. Many teenagers with DCD are actually really good on stage.

- Computing: if you've had to depend on word processing for school or college, you could deepen your knowledge or take up web design.

- Some computer games are great for spatial awareness and depth perception. If you have a Playstation, save up for the Dance Mat. One of the Colditz inmates got me to try out this amazing invention and although I looked like I was having a fit at first, as I tried to get my legs working, it really does help – besides being hilarious. Angela has muscle problems because of her Chronic Fatigue Syndrome, so I don't feel self-conscious in front of her. She's as awful as me. (I'm now being attacked with a walking stick for saying that!)

- Girl Guides and Boy Scouts: even the revamped 'let's-get-cool-and-modern' version of these organizations still offers challenges and activities to everyone.

- Volunteer work: as a dyspraxic person, you may be very compassionate and have a knack for empathizing with others. Don't selfishly hog special skills to yourself. Share them out.

No man is an island

Dealing with feelings of loneliness

Sometimes it must feel like you're the only dyspraxic person on the planet. Even the statistics – 'approximately 4 per cent of the population is affected by dyspraxia' (Dyspraxia Foundation) – don't do much to banish the mood of isolation that hangs over you like a storm cloud that never quite bursts.

Lots of teenage social environments aren't great for us. I would never be able to cope with the noise, smells, and crush of people in pubs and nightclubs. My idea of a terrible night out would be to teeter about in a pair of excruciatingly high shoes, surrounded by pointless babble and the blare of music that is too loud to appreciate. As there aren't many teenagers who rush off to the library at every opportunity, my social activity can be limited! But solitude doesn't have to be the same thing as loneliness.

When I first came to Colditz one of my roommates offered to accompany me into the common room, where everyone was having a riotous slipper fight. Standing in the centre of a crowd of people and pretending to be absolutely enthralled by what they are doing is much more depressing than sitting alone in your room with a mug of hot chocolate and a good book. Why do people assume that there is only one way to have fun? I would never force anyone to gleefully pore over Noam Chomsky's linguistic theories with me, so why should they drag me into a bar? Never do anything that you are uncomfortable with. You will be much happier if you are true to your own personality but spend more time either by yourself or with others who accept that your idea of fun might not always be theirs.

Liane Holliday Willey expresses this perfectly in her book *Pretending to Be Normal: Living with Asperger's Syndrome* (1999). She writes that you should always 'make time for fun, however you define it'. All this talk of therapy and treatment might have made you feel as if you have to redefine your personality in order to belong. Well, sometimes you just have to rewrite the dictionary instead.

The Dyspraxia Foundation has set up dozens of support groups across the United Kingdom. They host get-togethers where you can meet people with similar problems. A lack of social skills isn't such an obstacle when we're talking to other dyspraxic people. We're all in the same (somewhat leaky) boat and we can look beyond the disability to see the person. If there is no support group specifically for DCD in your area, you could join one aimed at dyslexic people. DCD and dyslexia often overlap and even if the people at the dyslexia group can't directly relate to your problems, they will know how it feels to be a bit different. Finally, we at the Dyspraxic Teens' website are always waiting to welcome new blood. (That makes us sound a bit vampire-ish, but never mind.)

CHAPTER 11

Lying Diagonally in a Parallel Universe

When we lose the right to be different, we lose the privilege to be free.

Charles Evans Hughes

Your future path

At the moment I still don't have much idea about where I want to go in life. All I know is that language and literature will be involved, because they are obsessions that I could never live without. For someone with DCD, choosing a career might not be easy. You may have been bullied throughout secondary school and have enjoyed little or no social life. Your teachers may not have been as sympathetic as they could have been and you might have run into problems as a result.

There are jobs available for sixteen-year-old school leavers but they're normally menial. I am not being snobbish when I use that word. Most menial jobs are very practical and I know that I could never do them simply because of the co-ordination they require. You probably wouldn't get on very well with a job that is rooted in your ability to use your hands. Going on with education is probably the safest option for most of us. This doesn't mean you have to stew in a classroom or go to university. You learn in your own way.

In the chapters 'Making the Grade' and 'A Survival Guide to School' I talked a lot about exams, perhaps making it sound as if you can't be successful without a string of qualifications after your name. When I was in primary school a classmate whom I didn't know very well told me that I'd end up doing a crap job, seeing as how I was a spastic. The incident happened years ago but it still remains very clear in my mind, and because of this I would hate anyone with DCD to give up on school because they wrongly believe they're no good. But not everyone enjoys studying and not everyone wants an academic-type job. There is nothing wrong with choosing a vocational course or deciding to leave school. Just make sure you are doing so for the right reasons, not because other people think you aren't up to much.

While you are deciding, you should take your weaknesses and your strengths into account. Will the course or job require you to do things that you find especially difficult? Will it allow you to make full use of your abilities? Because of the difficulties we have in some areas our skills are forced to grow stronger. Bearing in mind the nature of our problems, the obvious list of potential careers screams out…professional tennis player!

Er, not. Sorry, this book is nearly finished and I'm in high spirits because it's by far the most ambitious project I've ever done! To continue (seriously this time) dyspraxic people are often very strong verbally. Teaching a favourite subject, writing, librarianship, translating and counselling are all possibilities. If your brain has a creative twist you could aim for something theatre-related. If you have the typical dyspraxic ability to empathize with others, you could become a therapist or care worker. If you lean towards autism and prefer computers to coping with human beings then IT is an open door – you may have come to rely heavily on computers to dodge handwriting problems and you could use this knowledge to your advantage.

The majority of those jobs allow you to work alone or in small groups, if your social skills are not too good, or with a larger number of people if you choose to do so. They are flexible enough for you not to be harried by organizational tasks but structured enough to keep you within the confines of a safe routine. Remember that I am not all-knowing (though I might have fooled you for a while!) and the list isn't perfect or definitive. You might have a career aspiration not on the list, but if you have no idea what you want to do with yourself, these ideas are worth considering.

University applications and CVs

The first problem that a dyspraxic applicant is likely to face is filling in forms and completing all the paperwork neatly. Anyone from a parent to a special teacher to the Disabled Employment Adviser at the local job centre could help you to prepare a UCAS form or job application.

If you want to do this yourself, photocopy the forms several times. Use the first copy to work out how you will organize, space out, and present your information. Check how many words can fit onto each line. On the next rough draft decide whether the information you have included is relevant, and whether you could perhaps word it better. Copy it out again, working on spelling, grammar, and vocabulary. Now when you make your best copy all you have to do is focus on keeping your handwriting neat and legible without worrying about the content.

When you're applying for a job or a university place you have to 'sell yourself' without appearing too desperate to be there. When you're writing your personal statement or job application, you should:

- Grab the mysterious 'man behind the desk' with a thoughtful, interesting and relevant opening paragraph. (Easier said than done, as I have just found out!)

- Keep your information to the point. If you're applying for a job in computing, will your employers really want to hear about what a mean ginger cake you can bake?

- Work out what key skills the job or university is looking for, and then show that you've got them. For instance, 'Two years with the Naval Cadets, leading to a BTEC qualification, has equipped me with the sense of teamwork that the job requires'.

- Make sure that your language is precise and clear-cut. Avoid clichés and an overly chatty writing style. At the other extreme, don't put in complicated sentence structures and vocabulary that you wouldn't ordinarily use just to make a good impression. Your writing will sound stilted and unnatural if you do this.

- Check that your handwriting is legible! Maybe typing your CV or personal statement would be better. Don't forget to sign your name in a good-quality pen. This lends a personal touch to your writing. No one wants to think they're going to employ a robot.

Interviews

- Do your research before you go for the interview. If the organization is big, request information about its stance on specific learning difficulties. What support would be available to you?

- Send a very short piece of information on dyspraxia to the interviewer if you think they need it, so they will understand that you may need a little more time to answer questions.

- Prepare your clothes for the interview in advance. If you're applying for a job in a casual clothes shop, you won't be expected to turn up in a suit, but if you're being interviewed for an office post you will need to be a little more formal. The clothes should be comfortable as well as appropriate, and if at all possible made from a material that you don't find disgusting. It will be off-putting to the interviewer if you sit through the whole thing desperate to rip off your jacket and scratch!

- Read the guidelines that the university or company has sent you. What type of questions are you going to face? Is there a written test? If there is, tell the interviewers of your dyspraxia well in advance – you may have to type it.

- Get someone to give you a mock interview. Ask them to help you with body language, eye contact, voice control etc., as well as working with you on the way you respond to questions.

- Check that you know the location and time of the interview. Do a test run beforehand if possible, so you can fix landmarks in your head and work out how long it will take you to travel there.

- To prevent last-minute panic, make sure you have the correct money for the journey before you leave the house.

- Have a business card with your address and phone number on it to give to the interviewer. You may even forget the name of the road where you've lived for the past ten years when you're nervous.

- Ask someone to go with you if you get lost and disorientated easily.

- Have a long, refreshing sleep the night before. Wash your hair and eat breakfast. You need to look and feel your best.

- At the interview, smile when you greet the interviewer. If they offer to shake hands, do so. Remember that this isn't a police interrogation!

- Make sure your body language is relaxed and confident. People who don't have any postural difficulties slouch when they can't be bothered with something, so try to sit up straight.

- Don't be afraid to ask questions, but be careful to phrase them politely.

- Make sure that your responses are a decent length. Don't talk on and on, but don't answer in monosyllables. This is something you can practise.

- Finish on a polite note with a, 'Thank you very much'.

The first thing to do when you take up your place at university or accept a job is to scan the situation for potential problems. Look at the layout of the buildings. Are you going to be able to find your way around, or will you need a guide? Are there machines like photocopiers that you are unable to handle? Do you have to manage your time much more strictly than you did before?

If you're lucky the negative aspects of dyspraxia won't affect your job. If there are some snags that might trip you up, you should talk to your employers. Often you'll get the opportunity to talk about possible difficulties during the interview. But if you go in there and reel off a huge list of problems, people probably will think twice about employing you. You need to discuss the positive side of dyspraxia as well as the difficulties you face. Mention any special skills that you have, such as the ability to think originally ('It's got me used to approaching things in a very unique way that's just as effective – I think it will actually benefit my performance.') or your typing skills ('I can't write clearly, so I've become very proficient with computers and IT.') Now it's time to drop in the difficulties that you have. Suggest accommodations and assistance that your employer could give you. He or she will then realize that you aren't asking for the moon, or even for the place to be ripped down and rebuilt to your specifications, and they will also see that you are a responsible person.

The Disability Discrimination Act

According to the Disability Discrimination Act, a person with a disability is someone who has 'a physical or mental impairment which has severe long-term adverse effect on a person's ability to carry out normal day to day activities'.

A normal day-to-day activity for a thirty-year-old woman will be a little different from a normal day-to-day activity for a teenager. For instance, we are forced to run around a sports pitch in the blistering cold, fighting to get our limbs under control while PE teachers and so-called 'teammates' yell at us, and this is called normal. It's at times like this that I really do feel as if I come from a different planet, and frankly I like mine better!

Unfortunately the Disability Discrimination Act can't get you out of games lessons (damn) but it can fish you out of trouble when you start work. The government recognizes dyspraxia as a valid medical disorder, as defined by the World Health Organization's International Classification of Disease (hold it! Disease?) and if it's good enough for the government and the WHO, it should be good enough for any employer. The Act states that all reasonable adjustments must be made to help disabled workers, such as altering working hours to times when there aren't so many distractions, providing special equipment for the disabled employees to use, and arranging more training.

If your employer is prepared to follow these guidelines faithfully it's vital that you repay that trust. I like having rules to follow and am rigidly conscientious (apart from that one 'detour' I took just before a maths lesson...) so I don't really know about this temptation to skive that people sometimes suffer from. But I do have the logic to understand that if you take advantage of your differences, using them to get concessions or time off that you don't need, then the employer is going to start thinking, 'Oh, I won't have someone with that problem again'. All it takes is one lazy, selfish person to topple someone's good opinion of all of us. This sort of generalization may seem wrong, it probably is wrong, but for now this is the way the world works. Don't let the side down!

Tips for the workplace

- If you have to use machines or do tasks that require you to stick to a set of instructions, type the rules out and pin them up in several places. This will make sure that you never forget the right order in which to do things. It will also help everyone else who struggles with the same thing but is too embarrassed to say.

- Ask for a series of instructions to be given to you one at a time so that you can digest what you're being asked to do.

- Dust off your old memory techniques, like mind maps and mnemonics.

- If you're given a report or a big lump of text to read that you can't absorb, attack it with a highlighter. Pick out the key points and summarize it so that you get the gist of the document before you try reading the whole thing again.

- If you're dyslexic or have problems reading text when it is printed on white paper, substitute the paper in your printer for a soft pastel shade.

- Have a mini-whiteboard by your desk where you can jot down a to-do list – pictorially if necessary.

- Colour-code your filing system. Spend ten minutes per day organizing, sorting, and tidying to prevent a build-up of mess.

- Have one document tray for work you haven't yet started, one for work that's half-finished, and one for completed work.

- Gadget-ize your workplace or study centre with helpful pieces of technology. A talking calculator or clock, a timer, and a Dictaphone may all come in handy.

Dumping the distractions

- As I'm sensitive to noise I never knuckle down to work without my trusty earplugs.

- Put your mobile on 'silent' if you have one, mute the telephone, and switch on the answer phone instead.

- Politely ask people not to disturb you without good cause – building burning down, Martians parachuting onto university campus, etc.

- Do your work in a quiet area, far from hustle, bustle, and bright light.

- Try putting a screen around your desk if you have to share a very busy workplace.

Settling in

- Don't go home on your first weekend at university. Stay and try to make friends. Remember, everyone else will be as unsure and nervous as you are at first.

- Join a club or society that you are interested in so you can start to make friends.

- If there is a support group for students with learning difficulties, attend its meetings and get to know other people with your differences.

- Plan your time carefully so that you have a good balance between studying and socializing. Work is your first priority but don't shut yourself up by your desk all the time.

- Try not to obsess about home. If homesickness is a problem contact the university support services and see if they have a buddy system in place. Even if they don't, you will find that the other students are very sympathetic because they often get homesick themselves. I know this because of Colditz.

- Don't worry. If you had a hard time at secondary school or college this doesn't mean that your problems will stalk you through university.

Planning your time

Telling the time is very difficult for us, so how are we supposed to be able to plan it successfully? To do this, you need to make the concept mean something to you. I have a round orange cardboard clock that my mum helped me to make. It is divided into eighths and each segment represents an hour. I have several cardboard symbols that represent different things – the book means homework, the plate means tea. When I have homework I decide when I'm going to do it and I attach the cardboard book to the correct segment. I also stick coloured Post-It notes on this clock to remind me what I've got to do and when I need to do it.

- First of all decide on how long a particular task should take. You might have to ask someone else for help here, as gauging such an abstract concept isn't really a dyspraxic speciality.

- Use a buzzer to remind you of deadlines.

- If your tutor says she wants that essay in for 4 November, take the deadline forward and make yourself complete it earlier. In my experience you need a few days' grace to cope with unexpected emergencies – new assignments, forgotten assignments, computers that stubbornly refuse to print, etc.

- Timetable your day and get yourself into a comfortable routine.

- I always think that things will take me a shorter time to accomplish than they really do, and I end up worried and hassled as I frantically try to complete everything. If you build in extra time from the very beginning then this won't happen.

Day-to-day life with dyspraxia

Adolescents with learning difficulties become adults with learning difficulties. Cooking, cleaning, and managing your finances aren't easy tasks and the idea of moving beyond our safe planet can be frightening. How will I cope? This is the question that revolves in my brain like a stuck record. I am only two years away (I hope) from going to university myself and I have visions of myself running out into the street and propositioning a surprised passer-by with a tin opener and a can of food! 'And could you please help me to tie back my hair, too?'

I struggle to button up a duvet cover, iron my clothes (my arms always seem to get in the way) wash up a plate without smashing it, and organize my space, so it's no wonder that my mum often intervenes when I'm home from Colditz. 'I'll make up your bed, it'll only take me ten seconds,' and, 'Let *me* make you that cup of tea!' are examples of both her kindness and the painful truth: I, a sixteen-year-old, am incapable of performing tasks that the little kid across the road can manage with ease. In two years people will be calling me an adult and I want to taste some independence before then. But will my body let me?

This feeling of inadequacy is incredibly irksome and I have recently decided that from now on, I'll always make my bed, just as I do at Colditz. It takes me ten minutes rather than ten seconds, but I can do it. If I have to mop up an ocean of spilt tea from the kitchen surface whenever I brew a cup – well, I can handle that. Luckily I have never known what it's like to be 'normal'. If I had, everything really would be a nuisance in comparison!

It might be hard for some parents to accept that their little boy or girl is no longer so little, especially if he or she is still about as practical as a child. Adolescents with dyspraxia are often labelled as emotionally immature as well, probably because we haven't had the same social experiences as other kids. These differences won't stop your son or daughter from wanting to grow up and to take charge, and difficult as it may seem (especially where kettles are involved) you're going to have to trust us. And dyspraxic people, we have to learn to trust ourselves. Read through the rest of these strategies, kindly given to me by a number of adults with DCD, and good luck!

How to be a (dyspraxic) Delia Smith

Chapter 2, *The Hidden People at Home*, contains some useful tips on making your kitchen safe and improving your table manners. But when you leave home you will have to cook things in that kitchen (gulp) so here are some hints for preparing delicious – well, at least edible – food.

- Keep a whiteboard in your kitchen and write your shopping list on this. Add to the list each time you run out of an item, so you don't forget anything.

- Consider getting an occupational therapist to help you adapt your kitchen. Many OTs teach their clients some specialized cooking skills, such as how to multi-task in the kitchen – something that you will probably find very tough-going otherwise.

- Enrol in a cookery class.

- Plan your week's meals in advance. Work out what ingredients you will need for each meal and add them to your shopping list.

- Start collecting your own recipes. Cut recipes that you like the look of out of magazines, catalogues, etc. Keep them very simple to begin with.

- Rewrite recipes and break them down into simpler steps if you need to.

- Get out all the ingredients before you even begin to cook and arrange them on the worktop in the order that they will be used.

- Remember that oven and microwave cooking is more dyspraxic-friendly than frying and grilling.

- Turn saucepan handles away from the edge of the hob. You don't want boiling soup all over your feet.

- De-boning chickens is not easy. Don't buy whole chickens or turkeys but stick to frozen fillets, breasts, etc. that have already had the bones and innards and other delightful things removed. Boneless meat is easier to cut than meat on the bone.

- For better control when cutting or slicing, use scissors rather than carving knives – self-opening scissors are especially good.

- Use non-stick pans. These are much easier to wash afterwards.

- Make sure that healthy foods find their way into your fridge. Healthy food isn't just good for your body – it can alleviate some dyspraxic symptoms. If you have problems slicing vegetables (I managed to massacre my fingers with a carrot grater the other day) you can buy them ready peeled and sliced.

Shopping

- Purses and wallets can be a problem, particularly when you're trying to put your change away without dropping it, take your shopping, and put everything back in your bag. You end up going red and feeling burningly conscious of holding up the queue. Have a wallet or purse with a special section for pound coins, another one for silver, and a third for notes. Sort your money before you go into town.

- If you suffer from poor sensory integration, avoid crammed shopping centres with lots of bright lights and noise and smells. Go shopping when things are less busy.

- If you get lost easily it is better to shop in one self-contained mall than wander round several sprawling streets.

- If you find it hard to judge the passage of time, set a timer on your wristwatch to remind you how long you've been in a particular shop and how long you have left.

- Write out a shopping list to stop important things from slipping your mind once you are surrounded by noise and hubbub.

Oh no, the big 'O' (organization) – again

- Plan your chores. Take a few minutes out of each day to establish your goals, decide when you will do what, and give yourself a reasonable deadline.

- Break each room into small, manageable chunks and tackle one chunk at a time.

- Write down the sequence in which you will do the different jobs.

- Prioritize your tasks. Which ones need to be done now, and what can wait for another day?

- Try to get a reassuring friend to remind you of your goals.

- Take a five-minute break after completing each task.

- Minimalism is a style of décor that was probably invented specifically for people with organizational difficulties! The fewer ornaments and possessions cluttering up every available surface, the easier it will be for you to clean.

- Keep all 'like' things in the same place – tools in the toolbox, books on the bookshelf (unless, like me, you absolutely have to have a good supply of literature awaiting you in every room in the house) and cutlery in the cutlery drawer.

- Label cupboards and drawers to help you remember where different things belong.

- Find a special place to keep all the important items that keep going missing – glasses, spare keys, and so on.

- Have two document trays to help you sort out your post. Official correspondence goes in one, personal letters go in the other.

Cleaning

> My husband does all the ironing because he can't stand watching me struggle with it – also my hands have a number of scars from when I've lost concentration and ironed myself instead of the thing I was supposed to be ironing. I don't recommend doing that, it's quite painful!
>
> *Adult with dyspraxia*

- Clear the whole surface before you polish and dust it. Moving each object one by one is too much hassle and they will only break.

- A damp duster is better than a dry one, as you can spray the polish straight onto the duster.

- Work systematically over the surface, cleaning back and forth, back and forth, so you don't have to come back later to the patches you have missed.

- Use antibacterial wipes in the bathrooms and on kitchen surfaces as they clean and dry at the same time.

- Cylindrical vacuum cleaners are easier to lug around than upright ones.

A note to parents or housemates – if you're thinking of buying any new appliances, check that they are dyspraxic-friendly before you bring them home. Asking a dyspraxic person to vacuum the staircase when they can't manipulate an upright vacuum cleaner and are in danger of tripping over a trailing wire is a bit on the unsafe side. If you can't replace these appliances (though it's easier than replacing a human neck) then suggest that the person with DCD does things that aren't so lethal.

Driving a car

> Learning to drive was a big problem because I can't tell left from right and continually get mixed up. I decided to learn because my friends could all drive by their eighteenths and I didn't want to miss out. Judging the speed of oncoming cars is difficult and even though I did pass on my seventh attempt I avoid driving as much as I can. I don't feel safe.
>
> *Stacey, 20*

If you decide to learn to drive and you pass your test – congratulations.

If you don't manage to pass the test – cars pollute the environment. You are being friendly to trees and to the ozone layer by not driving and they appreciate your dyspraxia, even if you don't!

I will be sending off for my provisional licence when I turn seventeen and I'm determined to give this driving business a go, but it doesn't look too easy from the passenger seat. I have enough trouble crossing roads on foot so getting a car across might end up in disaster, but hey, you never know what you can do until you try! My dad has promised to let me take the car out into the desert when I'm in next in Saudi, but this doesn't sound sensible to me – even I could manage the desert, there's nothing there to hit.

Your driving instructors must (big emphasis) be aware of your disability. They won't refuse to teach you but they will be more attuned to your specific needs when you're in the driving seat. If you head straight for a tree they will realize that you probably think it is on the other side of the road and they will seize control long enough to rescue you both from a crash.

There are special centres dotted all over the country that are used to working with disabled learners, which assess us in a safe environment (i.e. not on a packed dual carriageway, which can only be good!) to establish our capabilities and make sure that driving is really suitable. Details of your nearest centre are available from the Mobility Advice and Vehicle Information Service. You can find their address at the back of the book.

- Try to learn in an automatic car. (Note: if you do this you will only ever be allowed to drive automatics in the future.) There are fewer things to think about and you can give your full attention to the road.

- Have extra wing mirrors fitted for easier parking and reversing. Personally I think that if you have depth perception problems it doesn't matter whether you have two mirrors or twenty – the problems are still not going to go away. But many dyspraxic drivers find this tip useful.

- Larger steering wheels are much easier to use.

- If you have problems with laterality, mark one side of the steering wheel with a sticker to remind you which is left and which is right.

- When taking the written test, request extra time.

- Plan your journey in detail to avoid getting lost. Clip directions to the dashboard.

- Ensure the directions are detailed enough for you. If you have laterality problems, then, 'Take the second left, followed by the third right' won't be much use. Request directions that are rooted in the surrounding landscape: 'Go down the street by the church, then take the road opposite the coffeehouse...'

- Use a reverse map so you don't struggle with left–right changeovers. You can even get voice-activated direction systems.

- Take frequent rest breaks if you can't concentrate for long periods of time.

- There are cars that make a sound if you get to close to another object.

- Pull over to a safe area at the roadside as soon as you are lost.

I have to ruefully admit that I'll probably never be allowed in a driving seat. If this is like you, too, then don't worry about it. We can't change who we are. Anyway, why would I need a car when I can fly a glider? I highly recommend it. My only problem is that I am not allowed to land one because of my lack of depth perception, but you do get a parachute!

Alternatives to driving

- Cycling improves both road sense and muscle tone, if you can overcome...

- ...problems with balance. It took me years to learn to cycle but the effort and the many tumbles were worth it in the end. Keep on persevering. Couple your efforts with physiotherapy and an activity like yoga or a martial art and you will have a better chance of mastering this (somewhat wobbly) mode of travel.

- Mirrors on your handlebars give you a greater command of the road.
- Make sure that the saddle is at the right height. When astride the bike, the soles of your feet should be resting flat on the floor.
- Have markers on your handlebars to help you tell left from right.
- Learn in a very flat area, such as a park. Take someone with you to keep you steady, or use stabilizers. Don't be afraid of looking ridiculous. The good citizens of Britain have seen stranger things than a teenager using stabilizers.
- If cycling is too difficult, ditch it for public transport. This seems to be getting a bit more reliable. Carry a copy of the timetable with you and familiarize yourself with the routes you travel most often.
- Using a bus pass or a season ticket is easier than having to sift through loose change whenever you get on board.

Disability Living Allowance

Some people with dyspraxia are entitled to financial benefit. To receive DLA you need a supporting letter from your doctor. There are two parts to DLA, mobility and care, and it is the care allowance (at the lowest rate) that people with dyspraxia are most likely to get. If you find it extremely difficult to prepare and cook a main meal you will be eligible for this. You should write a letter explaining exactly what you can't do (cut up vegetables, open cans, etc.) and why you can't do it, as well as detailing other aspects of daily life that you have difficulties with.

Only people who have real trouble walking two hundred to three hundred yards can receive the mobility component of this benefit. Most dyspraxic people can get across that distance easily, just not very gracefully, so it's unlikely that you will receive mobility allowance. However, if you can't cross roads because you find it impossible to judge distance and speed, have severe problems with orientation, and fall over a lot, you might be eligible for this. There is also a special benefit available from local education authorities – the Disabled Students Allowance, which is a grant for you to spend on specialized equipment at university or other things that you might need.

Touching the void

Leaving home and gaining independence may seem like a daunting idea at first. University? The very thought might terrify you senseless. Finding a job? Never, you might be thinking. The idea frightens even me sometimes, despite my…errr…indisputable wit and charm and zest for life. I'm nervous at the thought of adapting to a new lifestyle in less than eighteen months time when I haven't fully settled into sixth form yet. After six months I don't know my timetable. I still hate going into the sixth-form centre because of the noise. It seems that as soon as you have got used to something, wham! – you're off somewhere else. The earth turns too quickly.

You will probably have to take as much help as you possibly can. If you decide to leave home you might find looking after yourself a real challenge, but it's nothing that you haven't done before. I'm actually finding this time of my life easier than my first year at secondary school, probably because I have more choices now – I no longer have to strangle myself with a tie each morning and maths lessons are in their grave. The feeling of caged helplessness has evaporated because I now know that it's possible to cope with anything if you work at it for long enough. It isn't always easy, but nothing worthwhile ever is – no matter whether you are dyspraxic or not.

Thinking sideways

If a man does not keep pace with his companions, perhaps it is because he hears another drummer. Let him step to the music he hears, however measured or far away.

Henri David Thoreau, Walden

There are some things that make coping with our difference very hard. Sometimes, when I hear people chatting excitedly about their driving lessons or watch them jotting down a telephone number with ease, I feel a tremendous sense of bitterness. But then I remember that lying diagonally in a parallel universe means that we have a brilliant and unusual slant on life. We can see things that others can't, and for this reason I feel that we are very lucky to be dyspraxic.

When I see a child throwing a tantrum in a shop, I don't automatically think 'bad behaviour'. The child might have sensory dysfunction for all I know. When someone in the Colditz is feeling down, they usually find their way to my room – 'You always know how to cheer me up, Vic!' – not because I'm some kind of teenage Mother Teresa (a wimple would not do much for me) but because I know that to get anywhere you have to keep on running until eventually your feet leave the earth.

I can't pretend that the bad bits about life with a co-ordination disorder dissolve towards the end of adolescence. It is now October, and as I still haven't got enough co-ordination to blow my nose neatly I can expect to become a snot-spewing volcano as winter approaches. There are some aspects of DCD that the inspirational I-made-it-through stories will never tell you about, because they just aren't glamorous enough! But when you consider the gift of dyspraxia, you can overlook everything else – even waterfalls of snot.

If it weren't for dyspraxia I would never have written this book. I wouldn't be obsessed with language and my English ability would not be what it is. If it weren't for dyspraxia we would most probably be made to charge around an icy pitch at stupid o'clock on a November Saturday morning, frantically waving pieces of wood, our backsides turning blue with the cold and our frostbitten noses practically falling off. But as no one in their right mind is going to put a bunch of teenagers with all the co-ordination of a huddle of pregnant penguins on a hockey squad, we'll be warm in bed instead. For saving us from this fate, dyspraxia deserves a celebration.

I battled through…I am now in my final year at university, studying Multimedia Technology, plus, I am currently under-taking research into designing a Computer Aided Learning Application for children with dyspraxia. So I'm trying to help children with their education. I leave you with this message. Children who suffer from dyspraxia, don't give up. Try to prove to those teachers and peers that you are as bright as them, even brighter than them. It's like trial and error – IF NOT RIGHT, TRY AND TRY AGAIN. Go on. I know you can do it.

James, 21

'I've been with you all your life…'

There are people in this world who get a kick out of being cruel to others. We will continue to meet them throughout life. When you do, keep your head up high and think, 'I am not freakish or stupid, I'm unique'. Being polite to these idiots does not mean that you have to believe in or even acknowledge what they say. Luckily there will be lots of people who more than make up for them. Who knows? If the number of children with special needs continues to rise, we may one day find ourselves in the majority. And who will define the word 'normal' then?

I strongly believe that normality is all about personal perception. The one thing that everyone on earth has in common with each other is that we're all different to the person next door. For this reason I have to say here that even though you are right to be proud of yourself and of your hard-won achievements, the idea that teenagers with dyspraxia are somehow better than neurotypical adolescents is as dangerous and wrong as the notion that we are inferior to the rest. Treat others as you would like to be treated and always look for the best in them. Remember, if you do not look you will never see.

We are dyspraxic, but we are FANTASTIC! We are weird…and WONDERFUL!

Ruby, 12

That just about hits the nail on the head, as my dad would say!

I have now accepted that we will go through life hearing another drummer. The music we hear may cause us to march out of step, to fall behind everyone else, or even to race far ahead. Is this a bad thing? It could be – it all depends on how you treat it and what you are determined to make of it. To others we may appear disadvantaged because we struggle so much with various aspects of living and learning, but they can't hear the music we hear. I myself only really started listening to it on the day I finally woke up and stopped comparing myself to the regular world. Then I realized what an exhilarating song ours actually is. And I hope that one day, with our understanding and thoughtfulness and a helping hand whenever it needs it, the rest of the world will be able to appreciate our music too.

'If dyspraxia could talk to me it'd say…'

My name is dyspraxia – I've been with you all your life,
I've seen you go through a lot of pain and strife,
I can be your worst enemy, but I can be your best friend too,
I've made you what you are today – I've made you, you.

Please don't ignore me and hope I'll go away,
You have to face up to me every single day,
People think you're stupid, clumsy, lazy, or bad,
But it's me that taught you not to let those idiots make you sad.

Please don't feel clumsy when you break that cup,
Please don't feel useless and think you should give up,
Please have the sense of humour to laugh until you shake,
It's me that gave you that ability to laugh at your mistakes.

Please don't feel stupid when you fail that test,
Please understand you learn differently to the rest,
Please revise your way until you get it right,
It's me that gave you the ability to work with all your might.

Please understand when others do things wrong,
You know how they feel, so tell them to carry on,
Please stay polite even when it's hard to do,
It's me that's made you care so much for others as well as for you.

My name is dyspraxia – I've been with you all your life,
I've seen you go through a lot of pain and strife,
I can be your worst enemy but I can be your best friend too,
I've made you what you are today. I've made you, you.

Charlotte, 16

Acknowledgements

The acknowledgements section usually comes at the beginning of the book, but here in the parallel universe we do things differently. Now that you have gone on a walk through a dyspraxic world and hopefully been helped and entertained by what you found there, please take time to read about the people who made it possible for me to unwrap the gift of dyspraxia. Without them, this book would still be stuck in my head and I would still be trapped in the cage:

- Mr and Mrs Smith and Mrs Heyes, key-keepers of Colditz, whose trust made all the difference. They slid back the first bolt by convincing me that far from being useless, I actually verge on the terrific.

- Mum and Dad, who realized this fact long before I did. My new never-say-never philosophy is summed up with these immortal words: 'Three people more than enough for a quartet, anyhow!'

- The neurologist Dr Pam Tomlin, who formally introduced me to my brain, and the clinical psychologist Carys Pritchard, who helped me to make sense of it.

- My special needs teacher, Mrs A, who puts up with the aforementioned brain and demolishes the chaos. 'Dyspraxia is not an imperfection, it's just a different way of thinking!'

- Mrs Gault, who was canny enough to perk up Pythagoras with poetry. I can almost overlook the fact that you are a maths teacher.

- The resident dragon, Mrs Copland, who deserves the Victoria Cross for entering a war zone (my room) at great personal risk and helping me to tidy up.

- Lauren 'Gingerbread' Aspden, Kerry Bargelli, Angela (hatched any plans yet?) Loxham, Anna Li, and the rest of the Colditz chain-gang, who are always on hand to help whenever I get stuck in a toilet/lose my French homework/twist a few limbs...

- My roommate Shoop, who brightened up these pages with her artistic flair and said 'special' instead of weird.

- The formidable Kate Denham ('So many boys, so little time!') who spearheaded the non-dyspraxic advice panel and continues to make my life much more interesting than it really needs to be!

- Jamie Hill ('If he speaks, shoot him!') who patiently guided me through the quadratics, supplies humour as required, acts as human earplugs in the sixth-form centre, and never ceases to be inspiringly irritating.

- Sobia Asad Zuberi (dare I mention the detergent?) who walked with me across the chasm and is the only person in Saudi Arabia worse at cooking than me. It's good to know I'm not alone, although I have no teeth left to express my appreciation for you after nobly tackling those chocolate brownies! If I did, I would tell you that you are the best friend anyone could want.

- Finally, the many dyspraxic teenagers who speak through this book. Amongst them are Matthew Alden-Farrow, his sister Clare (not dyspraxic but pretty cool anyway) Hannah G. Cornish, Shaun McLaughlin, Anthony Forrest, Christopher Braxton, Johanna Montague, Abby Lewis, Priya Bhattacharya, Tom Smith, James, Stuart, Joseph, Lucinda, Paul, Charlotte, Eleanor, Ruby, and everyone else at Dyspraxic Teens Online. I am especially grateful to Matt, Hannah, and Charlotte, both for their brilliant contributions and their continued interest and support. You are all proof that the phrase 'dyspraxic is fantastic' is much more than a cheesy cliché on a website.

- And last but not least (OK, so the last one wasn't final!) there is the God in Heaven who answered my prayers and who made me as I am.

I thank you all.

Vicky

Useful Addresses and Websites

Bullying

Anti-Bullying Campaign
185 Towerbridge Road
London SE1 2UF
Tel: 0207 378 1446

Childline
Freephone: 0800 1111
A free counselling service for children and teenagers who need to talk.

www.bullying.co.uk
UK-based website on overcoming bullying.

Driving

MAVIS (Mobility Advice and Vehicle Information Service)
Macadam Avenue
Old Wokingham Road
Crowthorne
Berks RG45 6XD
Tel: 01344 661000
This government organization offers advice to disabled motorists.

Education

CreSTed (Council for the Registration of Schools Teaching Dyslexics)
9 Elgy Road
Newcastle-upon-Tyne NE3 4UU
A list of schools that specialize in the teaching of dyslexic pupils, and some
that help children with DCD.

Education Otherwise
PO Box 7420
London N9 9SG
Tel: 0870 7300074
Advisory service for people who are home educating.

SKILL: National Bureau for Students with Disabilities
Fourth Floor
Chapter House
18–20 Crucifix Lane
London SE1 3JW
Tel: 0207 450 0602

The National Academy for Gifted and Talented Youth
The University of Warwick
Coventry CV4 7AL
Tel: 024 7657 4213
Website: www.warwick.ac.uk/gifted
An education service open to gifted and talented young people aged 11 to
19. It offers a variety of extracurricular courses pitched at higher levels,
ranging from creative writing to astrophysics; a career planning service;
online study groups; and an Internet forum. Check out entry requirements
on the website.

http://cando.lancs.ac.uk
A database of careers information relevant to young people with disabilities.

Special needs associations

AFASIC (Association for Speech Impaired Children)
34 Central Markets
Smithfield
London EC1A 9NH
Tel: 0207 236 3632
Gives support to children and teenagers who have differences affecting
speech and language, such as verbal dyspraxia and semantic-pragmatic
disorder.

The Dyspraxia Foundation
8 West Alley
Hitchin
Hertfordshire SG5 1EG
Tel: 01462 455052
Website: www.dyspraxiafoundation.org.uk
Gives detailed information on dyspraxia and has established dozens of local support groups. Also has an online shop.

The Dyscovery Centre
4A Church Road
Whitechurch
Cardiff CF14 2DZ
Tel: 029 2062 8222
Website: www.dyscovery.co.uk
A wealth of support and information for anyone connected in any way with learning difficulties. Has an online shop selling a range of products designed to make life easier for people with co-ordination disorders. Dyspraxic nirvana!

The British Dyslexia Association
98 London Road
Reading RG1 5AU
Tel: 0118 966 2677
Website: www.bda-dyslexia.org.uk
An in-depth resource on dyslexia that publishes leaflets, articles, fact sheets, and books. Gives details on assessments and aims for nationwide 'dyslexia-friendliness'.

The National Autistic Society
393 City Road
Stratford
London EC1V 1NG
Tel: 0207 833 2299
Website: www.nas.org.uk
Provides information and help for people with autism and closely related disorders, such as Asperger Syndrome.

DANDA (Development Adult Neurodiversity Association)
Westbere Road
London NW2 3RU
Tel: 0207 435 7891
For all those different minds out there!

Dyspraxia Connexion
Website: www.dysf.fsnet.co.uk
Charity campaigning to support dyspraxic people and raise awareness of co-ordination disorders. Has some information and a special club for teenagers.

The American Hyperlexia Association
Website: www.hyperlexia.org
Information on this rare and little-known autistic spectrum difference.

Renee Newman's Dyscalculia Resource
Website: www.dyscalculia.org
Masses of information on learning differences that affect mathematics.

Need to talk, chill, make friends, laugh, understand?

www.darlen.co.uk/dyspraxicteen
Internet forum for teenagers with dyspraxia and related differences. Run by teens, for teens.

www.matts-hideout.co.uk
One of the best dyspraxia sites around. Matthew Alden-Farrow, one of the contributors to this book, offers brilliant advice on everything from how not to fall over on an escalator to home education.

References and Further Reading

Blanco, J. (2003) *Please Stop Laughing At Me...* Avon, MA: Adams Media Corporation.

Chinn, S. (1998) *Sum Hope: Breaking the Numbers Barrier.* London: Souvenir Press Ltd.

Colley, M. (2000) *Living with Dyspraxia: A Guide for Adults.* Hitcham: Dyspraxia Foundation.

Collins Gem Guide to Body Language and Facial Expression (1999) London: HarperCollins.

Frank, R. (2001) *The Secret Life of the Dyslexic Child.* Emmaus, PA: Rodale.

Grandin, T. (1996) *Thinking in Pictures and Other Reports of My Life With Autism.* Vancouver, WA: Vintage Books.

Higgs, R. (2002) *Bullying: What Have I Ever Done to You?* Cambridge: Pegasus Elliot McKenzie.

Holliday Willey, L. (1999) *Pretending to be Normal: Living with Asperger's Syndrome.* London: Jessica Kingsley Publishers.

Jackson, J. (2003) *Multicoloured Mayhem: Parenting the Many Shades of Adolescence, Autism, Asperger Syndrome and AD/HD.* London: Jessica Kingsley Publishers.

Jackson, L. (2000) *Freaks, Geeks, and Asperger Syndrome: A User Guide to Adolescence.* London: Jessica Kingsley Publishers.

Kirby, A. and Drew, S. (2002) *Guide to Dyspraxia and Developmental Co-ordination Disorders.* London: David Fulton Publishers.

Moody, S. (2004) *Dyslexia: A Teenager's Guide.* London: Vermilion Publishers.

Nichol, T. (2003) *Stephen Harris in Trouble: A Dyspraxic Drama in Several Clumsy Acts.* London: Jessica Kingsley Publishers.

Stordy, J. (2002) *The LCP Solution: The Remarkable Nutritional Treatment for Dyslexia, Dyspraxia, and AD/HD.* Basingstoke: Macmillan

World Health Organization (1992) *International Statistical Classification of Diseases and Related Health Problems, Tenth Revision.* Geneva: World Health Organization.

Wrobel, M. (2003) *Taking Care of Myself: A Hygiene, Puberty, and Personal Curriculum for Young People with Autism.* Arlington, TX: Future Horizons.

Yeo, D. and Chinn, S. (2003) *Dyslexia, Dyspraxia, and Mathematics.* London: Whurr

Index